THE QUESTION OF GERMAN GUILT

The Question of German Guilt

The
QUESTION
of
GERMAN
GUILT

By KARL JASPERS

TRANSLATED BY E. B. ASHTON

GREENWOOD PRESS, PUBLISHERS
WESTPORT, CONNECTICUT

Library of Congress Cataloging in Publication Data

Jaspers, Karl, 1883-1969.
    The question of German guilt.

    Translation of Die Schuldfrage.
    Reprint of the 1947 ed. published by Dial Press, New
York.
    1. World War, 1939-1945--Causes. 2. Germany--
History--1933-1945. 3. World War, 1939-1945--Germany.
I. Title.
D742.G4J23 1978   940.53'11   78-5401
ISBN 0-8371-9305-2

Reprinted in 1978 by Greenwood Press, Inc.
51 Riverside Avenue, Westport, CT. 06880

Printed in the United States of America

10 9 8 7 6 5 4 3 2 1

Ladies and Gentlemen:

Those of you who sat in these rooms as students in recent years are now thinking, perhaps, Everything suddenly sounds altogether different; the cast has changed; the course of political events presents the figures—now these, now those—as puppets; as organs of power they recite their little verses; whichever way they talk, none can be trusted, for professors do not bite the hand that feeds them, either.

I can understand this distrust in all young people awakened to full consciousness during the past twelve years, in this environment. But I beg you in the course of your studies to keep an open mind for the possibility that now it may be different—that now there really may be truth at stake. You are the ones who are called upon, each to help in his place so that truth may be revealed. For the time being, listen to my conception of the situation of the sciences at the university, and examine it. It is as follows:

In some sciences you will hear scarcely anything different from the past years. There, scholars who remained true to themselves have always taught truth. You will have met many a teacher again who in tone of voice as well as in the contents and fundamental views of his lectures faced you the same as he was all through these years.

On the other hand, notably in the philosophical and political fields, you may receive a strange impression. There everything does indeed sound altogether different. True, if those who studied here before 1933 or even in the first years afterwards were to come back, they probably would note a coinciding basic attitude in many of us. But there, too, it may be possible to feel a change wrought by the upheavals of this decade. And the change of cast is a fact. Teachers who would expound the National-Socialist phraseology to you have vanished. Others have reappeared as old men out of the past, or joined as young ones in a metamorphosis to freedom and candor, while 'til now they had to wear masks.

Again I ask you: beware the premature conclusion that only the opposite of recent values is taught, that we are talking just as before though in reverse, fighting what used to be glorified and glorifying what used to be fought—that in either case, today as yesterday, the doctrine was a result of political compulsion and thus no real truth. No; at least it is not so in all places. Where it is, there would indeed be no essential difference. The way of thought would not have changed, only the direction of aggressiveness or mendacious glorification.

By our manner of teaching we professors will have to show that the radical difference—though also marked in certain contents—decisively lies in the very way of thinking. If what was taught before was propaganda, neither science nor philosophy, we are now not to adopt another point of view but to return to the way of thinking as a critical movement, to research which is true cognition. This can be suppressed. Given room, it grows out of the essence of human existence.

To be sure, all thought and research depend on the political situation. But the difference is whether thought and research are forced and used for their own purposes by the political power, or whether they are left free because the political power wants free research, a region free from its immediate influence.

Before 1933 we had permission to think and talk freely, and now we have it again. The present political situation is a military government, and a German government which, being set up by authority of the other, is itself not yet a democratic government but an authoritarian one. But neither by the military government nor by the German one is a line of thought and research imposed upon us. Both leave us free for truth.

Today this does not yet mean that we are free to pass discretionary judgments.

The situation as a whole does not permit entirely free public discussion of every decisive world-political question which now plays a part in the political struggle of the powers. This is a matter of course. Though it may be painful and not an ideal situation, political tact may at times exact silence on certain questions and facts everywhere in the world, in the interest of the most propitious solution. Truthfulness demands that we admit this, but no one has the right to lodge a complaint. Talking about all things as we like and please is license, anyhow.

Only what we say ought to be unconditionally true.

The political events of the day are not a topic for lectures at the university in the sense of our being engaged in politics. Criticism or praise of the actions of government is never the business of lectures—but the scientific clarification of its factual structure is.

The fact that we have a military government now means, without my having to say so in so many words, that we have no right to criticize the military government.

But all that denotes no repression of our research, only a firm compulsion to refrain from doing what is never our business: dabbling in political actions and decisions of the day. To me it seems that only malice would consider that a restraint of our research into the truth.

It means, rather, that we are free to try by all means, and in all directions, to discover the methodically explorable. We have the chances of discussion and of our manifold views, but we also run the risks of distraction and rootlessness.

This again does not mean that we have freedom to engage in propaganda. Propaganda might perhaps be tolerated if in line with the political aims valid today. At the university it would even then be a calamity. We do not have to capture truth by quick statements. We have to test, to weigh, to reflect, to debate to and fro and pro and con, to question our own assertions. Truth does not exist as merchandise ready-made for delivery; it exists only in methodical movement, in the thoughtfulness of reason.

What I have said so far applies to our university as such, to its doctrine and research. For our present course the suggested problems of tension are especially acute.

I want to speak to you about our situation, and so I shall constantly skirt the immediate actuality of concrete politics,

which is not and should not be our theme. Yet what we want
to ponder is a condition precedent for our judgment in politics
as well.

I want to speak from philosophical motives, for our own
enlightenment and encouragement. Truth shall help us find
our way.

For these considerations we shall first visualize two necessities, the consciousness of which I deem particularly indispensable to Germans in our present situation. We must learn
to talk with each other, and we mutually must understand
and accept one another in our extraordinary differences.
These differences are so great that in borderline cases we
appear to each other like people of different nations.

TALKING WITH EACH OTHER

We have to get our spiritual bearings in Germany, with one
another. We have no common ground yet. We are seeking
to get together.

Talk from the platform is necessarily one-sided. We do
not converse here. Yet what I expound to you has grown out
of the "talking with each other" which all of us do, each in
his own circle. The manner in which this takes place everywhere is the ethos of the atmosphere we live in.

Everyone must deal in his own way with the thoughts I
expound. He is not simply to accept as valid but to weigh,
nor simply to oppose but to test, visualize and examine.

We want to learn to talk with each other. That is to say,
we do not just want to reiterate our opinions but to hear
what the other thinks. We do not just want to assert but to

reflect connectedly, listen to reasons, remain prepared for a new insight. We want to accept the other, to try to see things from the other's point of view; in fact, we virtually want to seek out opposing views. To get at the truth, an opponent is more important than one who agrees with us. Finding the common in the contradictory is more important than hastily seizing on mutually exclusive points of view and breaking off the conversation as hopeless.

It is so easy to stand with emotional emphasis on decisive judgments; it is difficult calmly to visualize and to see truth in full knowledge of all objects. It is easy to break off communication with defiant assertions; it is difficult ceaselessly, beyond assertions, to enter on the ground of truth. It is easy to seize an opinion and hold on to it, dispensing with further cogitation; it is difficult to advance step by step and never to bar further questioning.

We must restore the readiness to think, against the tendency to have everything prepared in advance and, as it were, placarded in slogans. One requirement is that we do not intoxicate ourselves with feelings of pride, of despair, of indignation, of defiance, of revenge, of scorn, but that we put these feelings on ice and perceive reality. We must suspend such sentiments to see the truth, to be of good will in the world.

Yet this, too, applies to talking with each other: it is easy to think everything tentatively and never to come to a decision; it is difficult to make the true resolve in the lucidity of universally open thought. It is easy to shirk responsibility by talking; it is difficult absolutely, but without obstinacy, to maintain a resolution. It is easy always in a situation to take the line of least resistance; it is difficult, led by the absolute resolution through all mobility and pliability of thought, to stay on the determined path.

These difficulties let us go astray in opposite directions. We make no headway if we play off the aberrations on one side against those on the other. Nor is there a middle way. Rather, man's way to truth lies in the realm of the causes to which those aberrations are due. There we go when we can really talk with each other. To that end something must constantly remain in us that trusts the other and deserves his trust. Then, amidst discussion, that silence is possible in which men listen together and hear the truth.

Therefore we do not want to rage at one another but to try to find the way together. Emotion argues against the truth of the speaker. We want to affect no fanatic will, nor to outshout each other. We do not want to engage in melodramatic breast-beating, to offend the other, nor to engage in self-satisfied praise of things intended merely to hurt the other. We do not want to force opinions on one another. But in the common search for truth there must be no barriers of charitable reserve, no gentle reticence, no comforting deception. There can be no question that might not be raised, nothing to be fondly taken for granted, no sentimental and no practical lie that would have to be guarded or that would be untouchable. But even less can it be permitted brazenly to hit each other in the face with challenging, unfounded, frivolous judgments. We belong together; we must feel our common cause when we talk with each other.

When we talk aloud to each other, we merely continue what and how each individual inwardly talks to himself.

In this kind of talking none is the other's judge; everyone is both defendant and judge at the same time. All our talks are darkened by such accusations, by the moralizing which has for ages mingled with so many conversations and keeps dripping into our wounds like poison, whatever it may be aimed against. We cannot remove this shadow but we can make it constantly lighter. We can have the right impulse: we do not want to accuse, except in the case of definite crimes capable of objective determination and of punishment. All through these years we have heard other people scorned. We do not want to continue that.

But we always succeed only in part. We all tend to justify ourselves, and to attack what we feel are hostile forces with depreciating judgments or moral accusations. Today we must examine ourselves more severely than ever. Let us make this plain: in the course of events the survivor seems always right. Success apparently justifies. The man on top believes that he has the truth of a good cause on his side. This implies the profound injustice of blindness for the failures, for the powerless, for those who are crushed by events.

It is ever thus. Thus was the Prussian-German noise after 1866 and 1870, which frightened Nietzsche. Thus was the even wilder noise of National-Socialism since 1933.

So now we must ask ourselves whether we are not lapsing into another noise, becoming self-righteous, deriving a legitimacy from the mere facts of our having survived and suffered.

Let us be clear about this in our minds: that we live and survive is not due to ourselves. If we have a new situation, with new opportunities amidst fearful destruction, it has not been created by our own strength. Let us not claim a legitimacy which is not due us.

As today every German government is an authoritarian government set up by the Allies, so every German, every one of us, owes the scope of his activities today to the Allies' will or permission. This is a cruel fact. Truthfulness prevents us from forgetting it even for a day. It preserves us from arrogance and teaches us humility.

Among the survivors, among those on top, there are today, as ever, the outraged, impassioned ones, all thinking they are right and claiming credit for what has happened through others. The man who is well off, who finds an audience, thinks that this alone makes him right.

No one can avoid this situation altogether. Time and again, when we get on this path for an instant, we must make a real effort to find our way back to self-education. We are outraged ourselves. May outrage cleanse itself, may it stay with us as outrage against outrage, as morals against moralizing. We fight for purity of soul in struggling against the invincible in us.

That is true of the work which we now want to do together in this lecture course. What we have thought as individuals, or heard in conversations here and there, may partly be objectivized in a reflective connection. You want to participate in such connected reflections, in questions and attempted answers in which you will recognize what lies ready within yourselves or is already clear. We want to reflect together while, in fact, I expound unilaterally. But the point is not dogmatic communication, but investigation and tender for examination on your part.

Brainwork is not all that this requires. The intellect must put the heart to work, arouse it to an inner activity which in turn carries the brainwork. You will vibrate with me or against me, and I myself will not move without a stirring at the bottom of my thoughts. Although in the course of this unilateral exposition we do not actually talk with each other, I cannot help it if one or the other of you feels almost personally touched. I ask you in advance: forgive me, should I offend. I do not want to. But I am determined to dare the most radical thoughts as deliberately as possible.

In learning to talk with each other we win more than a connecting link between us. We lay the indispensable foundation for the ability to talk with other peoples.

If I anticipate that which is to become the theme of these lectures only at their very end: for us the way of force is hopeless, the way of cunning undignified and futile. Full frankness and honesty harbors not only our dignity—possible even in impotence—but our own chance. The question for every German is whether to go this way at the risk of all disappointments, at the risk of additional losses and of convenient abuse by the powerful. The answer is that this is the only way that can save our souls from a pariah existence. What will result from it we shall have to see. It is a spiritual-political venture along the edge of the precipice. If success is possible, then it will be only at long range. We are going to be distrusted for a long time to come.

Lastly, I characterize ways of remaining silent to which we incline and which constitute our great danger (I myself cannot refrain from accusing—at least not from a mental attack on the aggressive mentality).

A proudly silent bearing may for a short time be a justified mask, to catch one's breath and clear one's head behind it. But it becomes self-deception, and a trap for the other, if it permits us to hide defiantly within ourselves, to bar enlightenment, to elude the grasp of reality. We must guard against evasion. From such a bearing there arises a mood which is discharged in private, safe abuse, a mood of heartless frigidity, rabid indignation and facial distortions, leading to barren self-corrosion. A pride that falsely deems itself masculine, while in fact evading the issue, takes even silence as an act of combat, a final one that remains impotent.

Talking with each other is canceled too by speech which no longer speaks in private—speech which means to insult but not to hear an answer, waiting rather for the moment of face-slapping and secretly anticipates what in reality is fist and manslaughter, machine gun and bombing plane. Rage can distinguish only friend and foe for a life-and-death struggle, talks frankly with neither and does not see men as men, to get along with by being ready for self-corrections. We cannot be conscientious enough in illuminating this sort of conflict and rupture in our intercourse.

The Great Differences between Us

Talking with each other is difficult in Germany today, but the more important for that reason. For we differ extraordinarily in what we have experienced, felt, wished, cherished and done. An enforced superficial community hid that which is full of possibilities and is now able to unfold.

We cannot sensibly talk with each other unless we regard

the extraordinary differences as starting points rather than finalities. We have to learn to see and feel the difficulties in situations and attitudes entirely divergent from our own. We must see the different origins—in education, special fates and experiences—of any present attitude.

Today we Germans may have only negative basic features in common: membership in a nation utterly beaten and at the victors' mercy; lack of a common ground linking us all; dispersal—each one is essentially on his own, and yet each one is individually helpless. Common is the non-community.

In the silence underneath the leveling public propaganda talk of the twelve years, we struck very different inner attitudes and passed through very different inner developments. We have no uniformly constituted souls and desires and sets of values in Germany. Because of the great diversity in what we believed all these years, what we took to be true, what to us was the meaning of life, the way of the transformation must also be different now for every individual. We are all being transformed. But we do not all follow the same path to the new ground of common truth, which we seek and which reunites us. In such a disaster everyone may let himself be made over for rebirth, without fear of dishonor. What we must painfully renounce is not alike for all—so little alike that one man's renunciation may impress another as a gain. We are divided along different lines of disappointment.

That the differences come into the open now is due to the fact that no public discussion was possible for twelve years, and that even in private life all opposition was confined to the most intimate conversations and was often furtive among the closest friends. Public and general, and thus suggestive and almost a matter of course for a youth that had grown up in it, was only the National-Socialist way of thinking and talking.

Now that we can talk freely again, we seem to each other as if we had come from different worlds. And yet all of us speak the German language, and we were all born in this country and are at home in it.

We must not let the divergence faze us, the sense of being worlds apart. We want to find the way to each other, to talk with each other, to try to convince each other. Let us visualize a few typical differences.

There were our conceptions of events, differing to the point of irreconcilability: some went through the whole disrupting experience of national indignity as early as 1933, others after June 1934, still others in 1938 during the Jewish pogroms, many in the years since 1942, when defeat became probable, or since 1943 when it became certain, and some not until it actually happened in 1945. For the first group, 1945 was the year of delivery and new chances; for others these days were the hardest, since they brought the end of the supposedly national Reich.

Some radically sought the evil's source and took the consequences. They desired intervention and invasion by the Western powers as early as 1933; for they saw that now, with the gates slammed on the German prison, delivery could only come from outside. The future of the German soul depended on this liberation. If its destruction was not to be completed, it had to be freed as soon as possible by sister nations of Western bent, acting on a common European interest. This delivery did not take place. The way led on to 1945, to the most fearful destruction of all our physical and moral realities.

But this view is by no means general among us. Aside from those who saw or are still seeing the Golden Age in National-Socialism, there were opponents of National-Socialism who were convinced nonetheless that a victory of Hitler Germany would not result in the destruction of Germanism. Instead, they foresaw a great future based on such a triumph, on the theory that a triumphant Germany —whether immediately or after Hitler's death—would rid itself of the party. They did not believe the old saying that the power of a state can only be maintained by the forces which established it; they did not believe that terrorism would, in the nature of things, be unbreakable precisely after a victory—that after a victory, with the army discharged, Germany would have become a slave nation held in check by the SS for the exercise of a desolate, destructive, free-domless world rule in which all things German would have suffocated.

Another difference lies in the way of the ordeal which, although common to all of us, is extraordinarily varied in the kind and degree of its particular appearance. Close relatives and friends are dead or missing. Homes lie in ruins. Property has been destroyed. With everybody experiencing trouble, severe privations and physical suffering, it is still something altogether different whether one retains a home and household goods or has been ruined by bombs; whether he sustained his suffering and losses in combat at the front, at home, or in a concentration camp; whether he was a hunted

(20)

Gestapo victim or one of those who, even though in fear, profited by the régime. Virtually everyone has lost close relatives and friends, but how he lost them—in front-line combat, in bombings, in concentration camps or in the mass murders of the régime—results in greatly divergent inner attitudes. Millions of disabled are seeking a way of life. Hundreds of thousands have been rescued from the concentration camps. Millions are being evacuated and forced to roam. The greater part of the male population has passed through the prisoner-of-war camps and gathered very dissimilar experiences. Men have come to the limits of humanity and returned home, unable to forget what really was. Denazification throws countless numbers out of their past course. The suffering differs in kind, and most people have sense only for their kind. Everyone tends to interpret great losses and trials as a sacrifice. But the possible interpretations of this sacrifice are so abysmally different that, at first, they divide people.

The loss of a faith makes a tremendous difference. All of us have somehow lost the ground under our feet; only a transcendently founded religious or philosophical faith can maintain itself through all these disasters. What used to count in the world has become brittle. The believing National-Socialist, his thoughts even more absurd now than they were during the days of his rule, can only snatch at feeble dreams, while the nationalist helplessly stands between the immorality of National-Socialism, through which he sees, and the reality of the German situation.

Equally vast is the difference in kind and degree of our

guilt. No one is guiltless. We shall take up this question later.

But no one is beyond the pale of human existence, provided he pays for his guilt.

True, it is sensible for the individual, depending on his past, to curb and resign himself—it applies to individuals, not to the many, that they should perhaps be silent now, for the time being.

In Germany we have not only the differences between the peculiar attitudes based on the German fate. We also have here the party divisions which are common to all the West: the socialist and bourgeois-capitalist tendencies, the politicized creeds, the democratic will to freedom and the dictatorial inclination. And not only that; it may yet happen that these contrasts will be affected by the Allied powers, and work on us as on a now politically impotent, pliant, testing material.

All these differences lead to constant disruption among us Germans, to the dispersal and division of individuals and groups—the more so as our existence lacks the common ethical-political base. We only have shadows of a truly common political ground on which we might stand and retain our solidarity through the most violent controversies. We are sorely deficient in talking with each other and listening to each other. We lack mobility, criticism and self-criticism. We incline to doctrinism.

What makes it worse is that so many people do not really want to think. They want only slogans and obedience. They ask no questions and they give no answers, except by repeating drilled-in phrases. They can only assert and obey, neither

(22)

probe nor apprehend. Thus they cannot be convinced, either. How shall we talk with people who will not go where others probe and think, where men seek independence in insight and conviction?

Often the outstanding difference is simply one of character. Some people always tend to be in opposition, others to run with the pack.

Germany cannot come to unless we Germans find the way to communicate with each other. The general situation seems to link us only negatively. If we really learn to talk with each other it can be only in the consciousness of our great diversity.

Unity by force does not avail; in adversity it fades as an illusion. Unanimity by talking with and understanding each other, by mutual toleration and concession leads to a community that lasts.

What we have mentioned and shall develop in subsequent discussions are typical traits. No one needs to classify himself. Anyone who feels himself referred to does so on his own responsibility.

OUTLINE OF SUBSEQUENT DISCUSSIONS

We want to know where we stand. We seek to answer the question, what has led to our situation, then to see what we are and should be—what is really German—and finally to ask what we can still want.

It is only now that history has finally become world history—the global history of mankind. So our own situation can be grasped only together with the world-historical one. What has happened today has its causes in general human events and conditions, and only secondarily in special intra-national relations and the decisions of single groups of men.

What is taking place is a crisis of mankind. The contributions, fatal or salutary, of single peoples and states can only be seen in the framework of the whole, as can the connections which brought on this war, and its phenomena which manifested in new, horrible fashion what man can be. It is only within such a total framework that the guilt question, too, can be discussed justly and unmercifully at the same time. At the beginning, therefore, we place a theme which does not even mention Germany as yet: the generality of the age—how it reveals itself as technical age and in world politics and in the loss or transformation of all faith.

Only by visualizing this generality can we distinguish what is all men's due and what is private to a special group —or, furthermore, what lies in the nature of things, in the course of events, and what is to be ascribed to free human decision.

Against the background of this generality we seek, second, the way to the German question. We visualize our real situation as the source of our spiritual situation, characterize National-Socialism, inquire how it could and did happen, and finally discuss the guilt question.*

After the visualization of the disaster we inquire, third:

---

* Only this last section on the guilt question is published in the following pages, with the contents elaborated on and freed from the form of academic lectures.

what is German? We want to see German history, the German spirit, the changes in our German national consciousness, and great German personalities.

Such a historical self-analysis of our German being is at the same time an ethical self-examination. In the mirror of our history we see our aims and our tasks. We hear them in the call of our great ancestors and apprehend them at the same time by illuminating the historic idols which led us astray.

What we think of as German is never mere cognition but an ethical resolve, a factor in German growth. The character of one's own people is not finally determined until it is historically finished, all past and no future any more (like ancient Hellenism).

The fact that we are still alive, still part of history and not yet at the absolute end, leads, fourth, to the question of our remaining possibilities. Is there any strength left to the German in political collapse, in both political and economic impotence? Or has the end come in fact?

The answer lies in the draft of the ethos which is left to us—and if it were the ethos of a people deemed a pariah people in the world today.

Introduction

Almost the entire world indicts Germany and the Germans. Our guilt is discussed in terms of outrage, horror, hatred and scorn. Punishment and retribution are desired, not by the victors alone but also by some of the German emigrés and even by citizens of neutral countries. In Germany there are some who admit guilt, including their own, and many who hold themselves guiltless but pronounce others guilty.

The temptation to evade this question is obvious; we live in distress—large parts of our population are in so great, such acute distress that they seem to have become insensitive to such discussions. Their interest is in anything that would relieve distress, that would give them work and bread, shelter and warmth. The horizon has shrunk. People do not like to hear of guilt, of the past; world history is not their concern. They simply do not want to suffer any more; they want to get out of this misery, to live but not to think. There is a feeling as though after such fearful suffering one had to be rewarded, as it were, or at least comforted, but not burdened with guilt on top of it all.

And yet, though aware of our helplessness in the face of extremity, we feel at moments an urgent longing for the calm truth. The aggravation of distress by the indictment (of the German people) is not irrelevant, or a mere cause of anger. We want to see clearly whether this indictment is just or unjust, and in what sense. For it is exactly in distress that the most vital need is most strongly felt: to cleanse one's own soul and to think and do right, so that in the face of nothingness we may grasp life from a new authentic origin.

We Germans are indeed obliged without exception to understand clearly the question of our guilt, and to draw the conclusions. What obliges us is our human dignity. First, we cannot be indifferent to what the world thinks of us, for we know we are part of mankind—are human before we are German. More important, however: our own life, in distress and dependence, can have no dignity except by truthfulness toward ourselves. The guilt question is more than a question put to us by others, it is one we put to ourselves. The way we answer it will be decisive for our present approach to the world and ourselves. It is a vital question for the German soul. No other way can lead to a regeneration that would renew us from the source of our being. That the victors condemn us is a political fact which has the greatest consequences for our life, but it does not help us in the decisive point, in our inner regeneration. Here we deal with ourselves alone. Philosophy and theology are called on to illumine the depths of the question of guilt.

Discussions of the guilt question often suffer from a confusion of concepts and points of view. To arrive at truth, we must differentiate. I shall begin by drafting a scheme of distinctions that will serve to clarify our present German situation. The distinctions are, of course, not absolutely valid.

In the end, what we call guilt has one all-embracing source. But this can be clarified only by what is gained by means of the distinctions.

Our darkest feelings do not mind being trusted out of hand. Though immediacy is the true reality, the presence of our soul and our feelings are not simply there like given facts of life. Rather, they are communicated by our inner activities, our thoughts, our knowledge. They are deepened and clarified in the measure that we think. Feeling as such is unreliable. To plead feelings means to evade naively the objectivity of what we can know and think. It is only after we have thought a thing through and visualized it from all sides, constantly surrounded, led and disturbed by feelings, that we arrive at a true feeling that in its time can be trusted to support our life.

Scheme of Distinctions

Four Concepts of Guilt

We must distinguish between:

(1) *Criminal guilt:* Crimes are acts capable of objective proof and violate unequivocal laws. Jurisdiction rests with the court, which in formal proceedings can be relied upon to find the facts and apply the law.

(2) *Political guilt:* This, involving the deeds of statesmen and of the citizenry of a state, results in my having to bear the consequences of the deeds of the state whose power governs me and under whose order I live. Everybody is co-responsible for the way he is governed. Jurisdiction rests with the power and the will of the victor, in both domestic and foreign politics. Success decides. Political prudence, which takes the more distant consequences into account, and the acknowledgment of norms, which are applied as natural and international law, serves to mitigate arbitrary power.

(3) *Moral guilt:* I, who cannot act otherwise than as an individual, am morally responsible for all my deeds, including the execution of political and military orders. It is never simply true that "orders are orders." Rather—as crimes even though ordered (although, depending on the degree of dan-

ger, blackmail and terrorism, there may be mitigating circumstances)—so every deed remains subject to moral judgment. Jurisdiction rests with my conscience, and in communication with my friends and intimates who are lovingly concerned about my soul.

(4) *Metaphysical guilt:* There exists a solidarity among men as human beings that makes each co-responsible for every wrong and every injustice in the world, especially for crimes committed in his presence or with his knowledge. If I fail to do whatever I can to prevent them, I too am guilty. If I was present at the murder of others without risking my life to prevent it, I feel guilty in a way not adequately conceivable either legally, politically or morally. That I live after such a thing has happened weighs upon me as indelible guilt. As human beings, unless good fortune spares us such situations, we come to a point where we must choose: either to risk our lives unconditionally, without chance of success and therefore to no purpose—or to prefer staying alive, because success is impossible. That somewhere among men the unconditioned prevails—the capacity to live only together or not at all, if crimes are committed against the one or the other, or if physical living requirements have to be shared—therein consists the substance of their being. But that this does not extend to the solidarity of all men, nor to that of fellow-citizens or even of smaller groups, but remains confined to the closest human ties—therein lies this guilt of us all. Jurisdiction rests with God alone.

This differentiation of four concepts of guilt clarifies the meaning of the charges. Political guilt, for example, does mean the liability of all citizens for the consequences of deeds done by their state, but not the criminal and the moral guilt of every single citizen for crimes committed in the name of the state. The judge may decide about crimes and the victor about political liability, but moral guilt can truthfully be discussed only in a loving struggle between men who maintain solidarity among themselves. As for metaphysical guilt, this may perhaps be a subject of revelation in concrete situations or in the work of poets and philosophers, but hardly one for personal communication. Most deeply aware of it are those who have once achieved the unconditioned, and by that very fact have experienced their failure to manifest this unconditioned toward all men. There remains shame for something that is always present, that may be discussed in general terms, if at all, but can never be concretely revealed.

This differentiation of concepts of guilt is to preserve us from the superficiality of talk about guilt that flattens everything out on a single plane, there to assess it with all the crudeness and lack of discrimination of a bad judge. But in the end these distinct concepts are to lead us back to the one source, which cannot be flatly referred to as our guilt.

All these distinctions become erroneous, however, if we fail to keep in mind the close connection between the things distinguished. Every concept of guilt demonstrates (or manifests) realities, the consequences of which appear in the spheres of the other concepts of guilt.

If human beings were able to free themselves from metaphysical guilt, they would be angels, and all the other three concepts of guilt would become immaterial.

Moral failings cause the conditions out of which both crime and political guilt arise. The commission of countless little acts of negligence, of convenient adaptation of cheap vindication, and the imperceptible promotion of wrong; the participation in the creation of a public atmosphere that spreads confusion and thus makes evil possible—all that has consequences that partly condition the political guilt involved in the situation and the events.

The moral issue also involves a confusion about the importance of power in human communities. The obfuscation of this fundamental fact is guilt, no less than is the false deification of power as the sole deciding factor in events. Every human being is fated to be enmeshed in the power relations he lives by. This is the inevitable guilt of all, the guilt of human existence. It is counteracted by supporting the power that achieves what is right, the rights of man. Failure to collaborate in organizing power relations, in the struggle for power for the sake of serving the right, creates basic political guilt and moral guilt at the same time. Political guilt turns into moral guilt where power serves to destroy the meaning of power—the achievement of what is right, the ethos and purity of one's own nation. For wherever power does not limit itself, there exists violence and terror, and in the end the destruction of life and soul.

Out of the moral everyday life of most individuals, of the broad masses of people, develops the characteristic political behavior of each age, and with it the political situation. But the individual's life in turn presupposes a political situation already arisen out of history, made real by the ethos and politics of his ancestors, and made possible by the world situation. There are two schematically opposed possibilities here:

Either the ethos of politics is the principle of a state in which all participate with their consciousness, their knowledge, their opinions, and their wills. This is the life of political liberty as a continuous flow of decay and improvement. It is made possible by the task and the opportunity provided by a responsibility shared by all.

Or else there prevails a situation in which the majority are alienated from politics. State power is not felt to be the individual's business. He does not feel that he shares a responsibility; he looks on, is politically inactive, works and acts in blind obedience. He has an easy conscience in obeying and an easy conscience about his nonparticipation in the decisions and acts of those in power. He tolerates the political reality as an alien fact; he seeks to turn it cunningly to his personal advantage or lives with it in the blind ardor of self-sacrifice.

This is the difference between political liberty* and political dictatorship, conceived from Herodotus on as the difference between West and East (Greek liberty and Persian despotism). In most cases, it has not been up to the individual to say which will prevail. For good or ill, the individual is born into a situation; he has to take what is tradition and reality. No individual and no group can at one stroke, or even in a single generation, change the conditions by which all of us live.

---

* "Theses on Political Liberty" were published by me in *Wandlung*, No. 6, p. 460ff.

The consequences of guilt affect real life, whether or not the person affected realizes it, and they affect my self-esteem if I perceive my guilt.

(a) Crime meets with *punishment*. It requires that the judge acknowledge the guilty man's free determination of his will—not that the punished acknowledge the justice of his punishment.

(b) There is *liability* for political guilt, consequently reparation is necessary and further loss or restriction of political power and political rights (on the part of the guilty). If the guilt is part of events decided by war, the consequences for the vanquished may include destruction, deportation, extermination. Or the victor can, if he will, bring the consequences into a form of right, and thus of moderation.

(c) The outgrowth of the moral guilt is insight, which involves *penance and renewal*. It is an inner development, then also taking effect in the world of reality.

(d) The metaphysical guilt results in a *transformation of human self-consciousness before God*. Pride is broken. This self-transformation by inner activity may lead to a new source of active life, but one linked with an indelible sense of guilt in that humility which grows modest before God and submerges all its doings in an atmosphere where arrogance becomes impossible.

Force is what decides between men, unless they reach agreement. Any state order serves to control this force so as to preserve it—as law enforcement within, as war without. In quiet times this had been almost forgotten.

Where war establishes the situation of force, the right ends. We Europeans have tried even then to maintain some remnant of it in the rules of international law, which apply in war as in peace and were last expressed in the Hague and Geneva Conventions. The attempt seems to have been vain.

Where force is used, force is aroused. It is up to the victor to decide what shall be done with the vanquished, in line with the rule of *vae victis*. The vanquished can either die or do and suffer what the victor wants. As a rule he has always preferred to live (here are the roots of the fundamental master-servant relationship as profoundly illustrated by Hegel).

Right is the sublime idea of men who derive their existence from an origin which is secured by force alone, but not determined by force. Wherever men become aware of their humanity and recognize man as man, they grasp human rights and base themselves on a natural law to which both victor and vanquished may appeal.

As soon as the idea of right arises, men may negotiate to find the true right in discussion and methodical procedure.

True, what in case of a complete victory becomes right for the vanquished and between victor and vanquished, has thus far played only a very limited role in events which are decided by acts of political will. These events become the

(37)

fundament of a positive, factual law which is not justified through right.

Right can only apply to guilt in the sense of crime and in the sense of political liability, not to moral and metaphysical guilt.

But even the punished or liable party can recognize the right. The criminal can feel his punishment as his honor and rehabilitation. The one who is politically liable can admit that the living conditions he must accept now are facts determined by fate.

Mercy is what tempers the effect of undiluted right and of destructive force. The humanity of man senses in it a higher truth, than may be found in the unswerving consistency of either right or force.

(a) Notwithstanding the existence of right, mercy works to open a realm of justice freed from flaws. For all human norms are full of flaws and injustice in their consequences.

(b) Notwithstanding the possibility of force, the victor shows mercy. He may be motivated by expedience, because the vanquished can serve him, or by magnanimity, because his sense of power and stature is raised by letting the vanquished live; or he may in conscience submit to the demands of a universally human natural law, by which the vanquished is no more stripped of all rights than is the criminal.

WHO JUDGES, AND WHO OR WHAT IS JUDGED?

The hail of charges moves us to ask: "Who—whom?" An accusation is meaningful only if it is defined by point of view and object and does not cross these bounds; and it is clear only if it is known who accuses and who is accused.

(a) Let us first be guided by an enumeration of four types of guilt. The accused either hears himself *charged from without*, by the world, or *from within*, by his own soul.

From without, the charges are meaningful only in regard to crimes and political guilt. They are raised with the intention of effecting punishment and holding liable. Their validity is legal and political, neither moral nor metaphysical.

From within, the guilty hears himself charged with moral failure and metaphysical weakness—and, if these led to political and criminal acts or omissions, with those as well.

Morally man can condemn only himself, not another—or, if another, then only in the solidarity of charitable struggle. No one can morally judge another. It is only where the other seems to me like myself that the closeness reigns which in free communication can make a common cause of what finally each does in solitude.

The assertion of another's guilt cannot refer to his conviction, only to certain acts and modes of behavior. While in individual judgment we try to take motives and convictions into consideration, we can truthfully do so only insofar as they can be established by objective indications, i.e., acts and behavior.

(b) The question is in which sense can a *group* be judged, and in which sense only can an *individual*. It clearly makes sense to hold all citizens of a country liable for the results of actions taken by their state. Here a group is affected, but the liability is definite and limited, involving neither

(39)

moral nor metaphysical charges against the individuals. It affects also those who opposed the régime and its actions. Analogously there are liabilities for members in organizations, parties, groups.

For crimes one can punish only an individual, whether he was acting alone or in concert with accomplices, each of whom is called to account according to the extent of complicity which as a minimum need not exceed the mere joining of such company. There are assemblages of gangsters and conspirators which may be branded criminal in their entirety, and in this case mere membership is punishable.

It is nonsensical, however, to charge a whole people with a crime. The criminal is always only an individual.

It is nonsensical, too, to lay moral guilt to a people as a whole. There is no such thing as a national character extending to every single member of a nation. There are, of course, communities of language, customs, habits and descent; but the differences which may exist at the same time are so great that people talking the same language may remain as strange to each other as if they did not belong to the same nation.

Morally one can judge the individual only, never a group. The mentality which considers, characterizes and judges people collectively is very widespread. Such characterizations —as of the Germans, the Russians, the British—never fit generic conceptions under which the individual human beings might be classified, but are type conceptions to which they may more or less correspond. This confusion, of the generic with the typological conception, marks the thinking in collective groups—*the* Germans, *the* British, *the* Norwegians, *the* Jews, and so forth *ad lib*.: the Frisians, the Bavarians, men, women, the young, the old. That something fits in with the typological conception must not mislead us to believe that we have covered every individual through such general characterization. For centuries this mentality has fostered hatred among nations and communities. Unfortunately natural to a majority of people, it has been most viciously applied and drilled into the heads with propaganda by the National-Socialists. It was as though there no longer were human beings, just those collective groups.

There is no such thing as a people as a whole. All lines that we may draw to define it are crossed by facts. Language, nationality, culture, common fate—all this does not coincide but is overlapping. People and state do not coincide, nor do language, common fate and culture.

One cannot make an individual out of a people. A people cannot perish heroically, cannot be a criminal, cannot act morally or immorally; only its individuals can do so. A people as a whole can be neither guilty nor innocent, neither in the criminal nor in the political (in which only the citizenry of a state is liable) nor in the moral sense.

The categorical judgment of a people is always unjust. It presupposes a false substantialization and results in the debasement of the human being as an individual.

A world opinion which condemns a people collectively is of a kind with the fact that for thousands of years men have thought and said, "The Jews are guilty of the Crucifixion." Who are "the Jews"? A certain group of religious and political zealots whose relative power among the Jews of that time, in cooperation with the Roman occupation authorities, led to the execution of Jesus.

That such an opinion will become a matter of course and overpower even thinking people is so amazing because the error is so simple and evident. One seems to face a blank wall. It is as though no reason, no fact were any longer heard—or, if heard, as though it were instantly and ineffectively forgotten.

— Thus there can be no collective guilt of a people or a group within a people—except for political liability. To pronounce a group criminally, morally or metaphysically guilty is an error akin to the laziness and arrogance of average, uncritical thinking.

(c) There must be a right to accuse and indict. *Who has the right to judge?* Whoever does so, exposes himself to questions about the source of his authority, the end and motive of his judgment, and the situation in which he and the man judged confront each other.

No one needs to acknowledge a worldly tribunal in points of moral and metaphysical guilt. What is possible in close, human relationships which are based on love is not permitted to distantly cold analysis. What is true before God is not, therefore, true before men. For God is represented by no authority on earth—neither in ecclesiastic nor in foreign offices, nor in a world opinion announced by the press.

If judgments are passed in the situation of a decided war, that on political liability is the absolute prerogative of the victor who staked his life on a decision in his favor. But one may ask (to quote from a letter): "Does a neutral have any right to judge in public, having stayed out of the struggle and failed to stake his existence and his conscience on the main cause?"

When the individual's moral and metaphysical guilt is discussed among people sharing a common fate—today among Germans—one feels the right to judge in the attitude and behavior of him who judges. One feels whether or not he speaks of a guilt weighing also upon himself— whether he speaks from within or from without, self-enlighteningly or accusingly, as an intimate seeking a way to the possible self-enlightenment of others or as a stranger and mere assailant, as friend or as foe. It is always only in the first instance that his right is unquestionable; in the second it is doubtful and in any case limited to the extent of his charity.

When it comes to political liability and criminal guilt, however, everyone has the right among fellow-citizens to discuss facts and their judgment, and to measure them by the yardstick of clear, conceptional definitions. Political liability is graduated according to the degree of participation in the régime—now rejected on principle—and determined by decisions of the victor, to which the very fact of being alive logically forces all to submit who wish to survive the disaster.

Defense

Wherever charges are raised, the accused will be allowed a hearing. Wherever right is appealed to, there is a defense.

Wherever force is used, the victim will defend himself if he can.

If the utterly vanquished cannot defend himself and wants to stay alive, there is nothing left to him but to accept and bear the consequences.

But where the victor cites reasons and passes judgment, a reply can be made even in impotence—not by any force but by the spirit, if room is given to it. A defense is possible wherever man may speak. As soon as the victor puts his actions on the level of right, he limits his power. The following possibilities are open to this defense:

(1) It can *urge differentiation*. Differentiation leads to definition and partial exculpation. Differentiation cancels totality and limits the charges.

Confusion leads to haziness, and haziness in turn has real consequences which may be useful or noxious but in any event are unjust. Defense by differentiation promotes justice.

(2) The defense can adduce, stress and compare *facts*.

(3) The defense can appeal to *natural law*, to *human rights*, to *international law*. Such a defense is subject to restrictions:

(a) A state which has violated natural law and human rights on principle—at home from the start, and later, in war, destroying human rights and international law abroad —has no claim to recognition, in its favor, of what it refused to recognize itself.

(b) Right, in fact, is with him who has the power to

fight for it. In total impotence, the sole remaining possibility is a spiritual appeal to the ideal right.

(c) The recognition of natural law and human rights is due only to the free will of the powerful, the victors. It is an act of insight and idealism—mercy shown to the vanquished in granting them right.

(4) The defense can point out where the indictment is no longer a true bill but *a weapon used* by the victor for other purposes, political or economic—by confusing the guilt concepts, by planting false opinion in order to win assent and ease one's conscience. Thus measures are justified as right, which otherwise would remain obvious actions of the victor in the situation of *vae victis*. But evil is evil even when inflicted as retribution.

Moral and metaphysical charges as means to political ends are to be rejected absolutely.

(5) The defense can *reject the judge*—either because there is reason to believe him prejudiced, or because the matter as such is beyond the jurisdiction of a human tribunal.

Punishment and liability—reparation claims—are to be acknowledged, but not demands for repentance and rebirth which can only come from within. Such demands can only be met by silent rejection. The point is not to forget the actual need for such an inner regeneration when its performance is wrongly demanded from without.

There is a difference between guilt consciousness and recognition of a worldly judge. The victor is as such not yet a judge. Unless he himself discards the attitude of combat and by confinement to criminal guilt and political liability actually gains right instead of mere power, he claims a false legality for actions which themselves involve new guilt.

(6) The defense can resort to *countercharges*. It can point to acts of others which helped to cause the calamity; it can point to acts of others similar to those which the vanquished are deemed, and indeed are, crimes; it can point to general world trends that bespeak a common guilt.

The German Questions

The guilt question received its universal impact from the charges brought against us Germans by the victors and the world. In the summer of 1945, when in all towns and villages the posters hung with the pictures and stories from Belsen and the crucial statement, "You are the guilty!" consciences grew uneasy, horror gripped many who had indeed not known this, and something rebelled: who indicts me there? No signature, no authority—the poster came as though from empty space. It is only human that the accused, whether justly or unjustly charged, tries to defend himself.

The guilt question in political conflicts is very old. It played a great part, for instance, in the arguments between Napoleon and England, between Prussia and Austria. The Romans may have been the first to introduce into politics the claim to their own moral right, and the moral condemnation of their opponents. Against this stands on the one hand the naïveté of the objective Greeks, and on the other the ancient Jewish self-indictment before God.

That condemnation by the victorious powers became a means of politics and impure in its motives—this fact itself is a guilt pervading history.

After World War I, the Treaty of Versailles decided the

war-guilt question, against Germany. Historians of all countries have since discarded the theory that only one side was guilty. At that time, as Lloyd George put it, all sides had "skidded" into the war.

Today things are altogether different. The question of guilt has acquired a more comprehensive meaning. It sounds quite unlike before.

This time the war-guilt question, in the foreground after 1918, is very clear. The war was unleashed by Hitler Germany. Germany is guilty of the war through its régime, which started the war at its own chosen moment, while none of the rest wanted it.

Today, however, "You are the guilty" means much more than war guilt.

That poster has by now been almost forgotten. But what we learned from it has remained: first, the reality of a world opinion which condemns us as a nation—and second, our own concern.

World opinion matters to us. It is mankind which so considers us—a fact to which we cannot be indifferent. Besides, guilt is coming to be a political weapon. Being held guilty, we have in this view deserved whatever grief we have come to, and are yet to come to. Herein lies the justification of the politicians who partition Germany, who restrict its reconstruction possibilities, who would leave it peaceless, suspended between life and death. The political question—which we do not have to decide and whose decision we can scarcely influence even by our most blameless conduct—is whether it is politically sensible, purposeful, safe and just to turn a whole nation into a pariah nation, to degrade it beneath all others, to dishonor it further, once it had dishonored itself. Here we are not discussing this question, nor the political question whether, and in what sense, it is necessary and useful to make admissions of guilt. It may be that the condemnation of the German people will stand. It would have tremendous consequences for us. We still hope that some day the statesmen will revise their decision, and the nations their opinion. Yet ours is not to accuse but to accept. The utter impotence to which National-Socialism brought us, and from which there is no escape in the present, technologically conditioned world situation, leaves us no alternative.

But even more important to us is how we analyze, judge and cleanse ourselves. Those charges from without no longer are our concern. On the other hand, there are the charges from within which have been voiced in German souls for twelve years, for moments at least, more or less clearly but impossible to overhear. They, by the changes they effect in ourselves, old or young, are the source of whatever self-respect is still possible for us. We must clarify the question of German guilt. This is our own business. It is independent of outside charges, however much we may hear and use them as questions and mirrors.

That statement, "You are the guilty," can have several meanings. It can mean:

"You must answer for the acts of the régime you tolerated"—this involves our political guilt.

Or: "You are guilty, moreover, of giving your support and cooperation to this régime"—therein lies our moral guilt.

Or: "You are guilty of standing by inactively when the crimes were committed"—there, a metaphysical guilt suggests itself.

I hold these three statements to be true—although only the first, concerning political liability, is quite correct and to be made without reservations, while the second and third, on moral and metaphysical guilt, become untrue in legal form, as uncharitable testimony.

A further meaning of "You are the guilty" could be:

"You took part in these crimes, and are therefore criminals yourselves." This statement, applied to the overwhelming majority of Germans, is patently false.

Lastly, the phrase may mean: "You are inferior as a nation, ignoble, criminal, the scum of the earth, different from all other nations." This is the collectivist type of thought and appraisal, classifying every individual under these generalizations. It is radically false and itself inhuman, whether done for good or evil ends.

After these brief anticipatory remarks we shall now take up the question at close range.

Differentiation of German Guilt

THE CRIMES

Unlike the case in World War I when we Germans did not need to admit specific crimes committed by one side only (a fact eventually recognized by scientific historic research even on the part of Germany's enemies), today the crimes committed by the Nazi government—in Germany before the war, everywhere during the war—are evident.

Unlike the case in World War I when the war-guilt question was not decided against one side by the historians of all nations, this war was begun by Hitler Germany.

Unlike World War I, finally, this war really became a world war. It struck the world in a different situation and in a different knowledge. Its import, compared with earlier wars, entered another dimension.

And today we have something entirely new in world history. The victors are establishing a court. The Nuremberg trial deals with crimes.

The primary result is a clear delimitation in two directions:

First, not the German people are being tried here but individual, criminally accused Germans—on principle all leaders of the Nazi régime. This line was drawn at the outset by the American member of the prosecution. "We want to make it clear," Jackson said in his fundamental address, "that we do not intend to accuse the whole German people."

Second, the suspects are not accused indiscriminately. They are charged with specific crimes expressly defined in the statute of the International Military Tribunal.

At this trial we Germans are spectators. We did not bring it about and we are not running it, although the defendants are men who brought disaster over us. "Indeed the Germans —as much as the outside world—have an account to settle with the defendants," Jackson said.

Many a German smarts under this trial. The sentiment is understandable. Its cause is the same which moved the other side to blame the whole German people for the Hitler régime and its acts. Every citizen is jointly liable for the doings and jointly affected by the sufferings of his own state. A criminal state is charged against its whole population. Thus the citizen feels the treatment of his leaders as his own, even if they are criminals. In their persons the people are also condemned. Thus the indignity and mortification experienced by the leaders of the state are felt by the people as their own indignity and mortification. Hence their instinctive, initially unthinking rejection of the trial.

The political liability we have to meet here is painful indeed. We must experience mortification if required by our political liability. Thereby, symbolically, we experience our utter political impotence and our elimination as a political factor.

Yet everything depends on how we conceive, interpret, appropriate and translate our instinctive concern.

One possibility is outright rejection of indignity. We look for reasons, then, to deny the right, the truthfulness, the purpose of the whole trial.

(1) We engage in general reflections: There have been wars throughout history and there will be more. No one people is guilty of war. Wars are due to human nature, to the universal culpability of man. A conscience which proclaims itself not guilty is superficial. By its very conduct such self-righteousness breeds future wars.

Rebuttal: This time there can be no doubt that Germany planned and prepared this war and started it without provocation from any other side. It is altogether different from 1914. Germany is not called guilty of war but of this war. And this war itself is something new and different, occurring in a situation unparalleled in the past history of the world.

This objection to the Nuremberg trial may be phrased in other ways, perhaps as follows: It is an insoluble problem of human existence that what must be settled by invoking the judgment of God, keeps pressing time and again for a decision by force. The soldier's feelings are chivalrous, and even in defeat he has a right to be offended if treated in an unchivalrous manner.

Rebuttal: Germany, throwing all chivalry overboard and violating international law, has committed numerous acts resulting in the extermination of populations and in other inhumanities. Hitler's actions from the start were directed against every chance of a reconciliation. It was to be victory or ruin. Now we feel the consequences of the ruin. All claims to chivalry—even though a great many individual soldiers and entire units are guiltless and themselves have always acted chivalrously—is voided by the Wehrmacht's readiness to execute criminal orders as Hitler's organizations. Once betrayed, chivalry and magnanimity cannot be claimed in one's favor, after the fact. This war did not break out between opponents alike in kind, come to a dead end and chivalrously entering the lists. It was conceived and executed by criminal cunning and the reckless totality of a destructive will.

In the midst of war there is the possibility of inhibitions. Kant's injunction, that nothing must happen in war which would make reconcilement flatly impossible, was first rejected on principle by Hitler Germany. As a result, force, essentially unchanged from time immemorial and with the measure of its destructive possibilities determined now by technology, is boundlessly with us. To have begun the war in the present world situation—this is the enormity.

(2) The trial is said to be a national disgrace for all Germans; if there were Germans on the tribunal, at least, then Germans would be judged by Germans.

Rejoinder: The national disgrace lies not in the tribunal but in what brought it on—in the fact of this régime and its acts. The consciousness of national disgrace is inescapable for every German. It aims in the wrong direction if turning against the trial rather than its cause.

Moreover: Had the victors named a German tribunal, or appointed Germans as associate judges, this would make no change at all. The Germans would not sit on the court by virtue of a German self-liberation but by the grace of the victors. The national disgrace would be the same. The trial is due to the fact that we did not free ourselves from the criminal régime but were liberated by the Allies.

(3) One counterargument runs as follows: How can we speak of crimes in the realm of political sovereignty? To grant this would mean that any victor can make a criminal of the vanquished—and the meaning and the mystery of God-derived authority would cease. Men once obeyed by a nation—in particular former Emperor William II and now "the Fuehrer"—are considered inviolable.

Rebuttal: This is a habit of thought derived from the tradition of political life in Europe, preserved the longest in Germany. Today, however, the halo round the heads of states has vanished. They are men and answer for their deeds. Ever since European nations have tried and beheaded their monarchs, the task of the people has been to keep their leaders in check. The acts of states are also the acts of persons. Men are individually responsible and liable for them.

(4) Legally we hear the following argument: There can be crimes only insofar as there are laws. A crime is a breach of these laws. It must be clearly defined and factually determinable without ambiguity. In particular—*nulla poena sine lege*—sentence can only be passed under a law in force before the act was committed. In Nuremberg, however, men are judged retroactively under laws now made by the victors.

Rebuttal: In the sense of humanity, of human rights and natural law, and in the sense of the Western ideas of liberty and democracy, laws already exist by which crimes may be determined.

There are also agreements which—if voluntarily signed by both sides—create such a superior law that can serve as a yardstick in case a contract is broken.

And the jurisdiction, which in the peaceful order of a state rests in the courts, can after a war rest only in the victor's tribunal.

(5) Hence the further objection: Victorious might does not make right. Success cannot claim jurisdiction over right and truth. A tribunal which could investigate and judge war guilt and war crimes objectively is an impossibility. Such a court is always partisan. Even a court of neutrals would be partisan, since the neutrals are powerless and actually part of the victors' following. To judge freely, a court would have to be backed by a power capable of enforcing its decisions against both disputants.

This argument, of the illusive nature of such justice, goes on to say that every war is blamed on the loser. He is forced to admit his guilt. His subsequent economic exploitation is disguised as restitution. Pillage is forged into a rightful act. If the right is not free, let us have naked force—it would be honest, and it would be easier to bear. In fact, there is nothing beside the victor's power. Recrimination as such can always be made mutual; but only the victor can make his charges stick, and he does so ruthlessly and solely in his own interest. Everything else merely serves to disguise the actual arbitrary force of the powerful.

And: The tribunal's illusive nature finally shows in the fact that the so-called crimes are prosecuted only if committed by a vanquished nation. In sovereign or victorious nations the same acts are ignored, not even discussed, much less punished.

Rebuttal: Power and force are indeed decisive realities in the human world, but they are not the only ones. To make them absolute is to remove all reliable links between men. While they are absolute, no agreement is possible. As Hitler actually said, agreements are valid only while they represent self-interest. (And he acted accordingly.) But this is opposed by a will which, admitting the reality of power and the effectiveness of the nihilistic view, holds them undesirable and to be changed at any cost.

For in human affairs reality is not yet truth. That reality, rather, is to be confronted with another. And the existence of this other reality depends upon the human will. Every man, in his freedom, must know where he stands and what he wants.

From this point of view it may be said that the trial, as a new attempt in behalf of order in the world, does not grow meaningless if it cannot yet be based on a legal world order but must still halt within a political framework. Unlike a court trial, it does not yet take place in the closed order of a state.

Hence Jackson's frank satement that "if the defense were permitted to deviate from the strictly limited charges of the indictment, the trial would be prolonged and the court enmeshed in insoluble political disputes."

This also means that the defense does not have to deal with the question of war guilt and its historical premises, either, but solely with the question who began this war. Nor does it have the right to adduce or judge other cases of similar crimes. Political necessity limits discussion. But this does not make everything untruthful. On the contrary, the difficulties, the objections, are candidly, if briefly, expressed.

There is no denying the basic situation: that success in combat, not the law alone, is the governing starting point. It is true in big as well as little things that—as ironically said of military offenses—you are not punished because of the law but because you got caught. But this basic situation does not make man unable to transform his power, after success and on the strength of his freedom, into a realization of the right. And even if this is not entirely accomplished, even if right ensues only to some extent, a great stride has been made on the way to world order. Moderation as such creates a zone of reflection and examination, a zone of clarity, and thereby makes men more fully aware of the lasting import of force as such.

For us Germans, the advantages of this trial are its distinction between the definite crimes of the leaders and its very failure to condemn the people as a whole.

But the trial means a great deal more. For the first time, and for all times to come, it is to make war a crime and to draw the conclusions. What the Kellogg-Briand pact began shall be realized for the first time. There is no more doubt of the greatness of this undertaking than of the good-will of many who have a hand in it. The undertaking may appear fantastic. But when the stakes become clear to us, the event makes us tremble with hope. The only difference is whether we gloat nihilistically, assuming that it could not but be a sham trial, or whether we passionately wish that it might succeed.

It all depends on how the trial is run, on its contents, its outcome, on the reasons adduced to the verdict—on the overall impression of the proceedings, in retrospect. It depends on whether the world can admit the truth and the right of what was done there, on whether even the vanquished cannot help concurring, on whether history later will see its justice and truth.

Yet this will not be decided in Nuremberg alone. The essential point is whether the Nuremberg trial comes to be a link in a chain of meaningful, constructive political acts (however often these may be frustrated by error, unreason, heartlessness and hate) or whether, by the yardstick there applied to mankind, the very powers now erecting it will in the end be found wanting. The powers initiating Nuremberg thereby attest their common aim of world government, by submitting to world order. They attest their willingness really to accept responsibility for mankind as the result of their victory—not just for their own countries. Such testimony must not be false testimony.

It will either create confidence in the world that right was done and a foundation laid in Nuremberg—in which case the political trial will have become a legal one, with law creatively founded and realized for a new world now waiting to be built. Or disappointment by untruthfulness will create an even worse world atmosphere breeding new wars; instead of a blessing, Nuremberg would become a factor of doom, and in the world's eventual judgment the trial would have been a sham and a mock trial. This must not happen.

The answer to all arguments against the trial is that Nuremberg is something really new. That the arguments point to possible dangers cannot be denied. But it is wrong, first, to think in sweeping alternatives, with flaws, mistakes and failings in detail leading at once to wholesale rejection, whereas the main point is the powers' trend of action, their unwavering patience in active responsibility. Contradictions in detail are to be overcome by acts designed to bring world order out of confusion. It is wrong, secondly, to strike an attitude of outraged aggressiveness and to say no from the start.

What happens in Nuremberg, no matter how many objections it may invite, is a feeble, ambiguous harbinger of a world order, the need of which mankind is beginning to feel. This is the entirely new situation. The world order is not at hand by any means—rather, there are still huge conflicts and incalculable perils of war ahead of its realization—but it has come to seem possible to thinking humanity; it has appeared on the horizon as a barely perceptible dawn, while in case of failure the self-destruction of mankind looms as a fearful menace before our eyes.

Utter lack of power can only cling to the world as a whole. On the brink of nothingness it turns to the origin, to the all-encompassing. So it is precisely the German who might become aware of the extraordinary import of this harbinger.

Our own salvation in the world depends on the world order which—although not yet established in Nuremberg—is suggested by Nuremberg.

For crimes the criminal is punished. The restriction of the Nuremberg trial to criminals serves to exonerate the German people. Not, however, so as to free them of all guilt—on the contrary. The nature of our real guilt only appears the more clearly.

We were German nationals at the time when the crimes were committed by the régime which called itself German, which claimed to be Germany and seemed to have the right to do so, since the power of the state was in its hands and until 1943 it found no dangerous opposition.

The destruction of any decent, truthful German polity must have its roots also in modes of conduct of the majority of the German population. A people answers for its polity.

Every German is made to share the blame for the crimes committed in the name of the Reich. We are collectively liable. The question is in what sense each of us must feel co-responsible. Certainly in the political sense of the joint liability of all citizens for acts committed by their state—but for that reason not necessarily also in the moral sense of actual or intellectual participation in crime. Are we Germans to be held liable for outrages which Germans inflicted on us, or from which we were saved as by a miracle? Yes—inasmuch as we let such a régime rise among us. No—insofar as many of us in our deepest hearts opposed all this evil and have no morally guilty acts or inner motivations to admit. To hold liable does not mean to hold morally guilty.

Guilt, therefore, is necessarily collective as the political liability of nationals, but not in the same sense as moral and metaphysical, and never as criminal guilt. True, the acceptance of political liability with its fearful consequences is hard on every individual. What it means to us is political impotence and a poverty which will compel us for long times to live in or on the fringes of hunger and cold and to struggle vainly. Yet this liability as such leaves the soul untouched.

Politically everyone acts in the modern state, at least by voting, or failing to vote, in elections. The sense of political liability lets no man dodge.

If things go wrong the politically active tend to justify themselves; but such defenses carry no weight in politics. For instance, they meant well and had the best intentions—Hindenburg, for one, did surely not mean to ruin Germany or hand it over to Hitler. That does not help him; he did—and that is what counts. Or they foresaw the disaster, said so, and warned; but that does not count politically, either, if no action followed or if it had no effect.

One might think of cases of wholly non-political persons who live aloof of all politics, like monks, hermits, scholars, artists—if really quite non-political, those might possibly be excused from all guilt. Yet they, too, are included among the politically liable, because they, too, live by the order of the state. There is no such aloofness in modern states.

One may wish to make such aloofness possible, yet one cannot help admit to this limitation. We should like to respect and love a non-political life, but the end of political participation would also end the right of the non-political ones to judge concrete political acts of the day and thus to play riskless politics. A non-political zone demands with-

of patently evil commands, it is a foundation of the sense of life.

But a soldier's probation must not be identified with the cause he fought for. To have been a good soldier does not absolve from all other guilt.

The unconditional identification of the actual state with the German nation and army constitutes guilt incurred through false conscience. A first-class soldier may have succumbed to the falsification of his conscience which enabled him to do and permit obviously evil things because of patriotism. Hence the good conscience in evil deeds.

Yet our duty to the fatherland goes far beneath blind obedience to its rulers of the day. The fatherland ceases to be a fatherland when its soul is destroyed. The power of the state is not an end in itself; rather, it is pernicious if this state destroys the German character. Therefore, duty to the fatherland did not by any means lead consistently to obedience to Hitler and to the assumption that even as a Hitler state Germany must, of course, win the war at all costs. Herein lies the false conscience. It is no simple guilt. It is at the same time a tragic confusion, notably of a large part of our unwitting youth. To do one's duty to the fatherland means to commit one's whole person to the highest demands made on us by the best of our ancestors, not by the idols of a false tradition.

It was amazing to see the complete self-identification with army and state, in spite of all evil. For this unconditionality of a blind nationalism—only conceivable as the last crumbling ground in a world about to lose all faith—was moral guilt.

It was made possible, furthermore, by a misinterpretation of the Biblical warning: "Let every soul be subject unto the higher powers"—a warning completely perverted by the curious sanctity appertaining to orders in military tradition. "This is an order"—in the ears of many these words had and still have a ring of pathos as if voicing the highest duty. But simultaneously, by shrugging off stupidity and evil as inevitable, they furnished an excuse. What finally turned this conduct into full-fledged moral guilt was the eagerness to obey—that compulsive conduct, feeling itself conscientious and, in fact, forsaking all conscience.

Many a youth nauseated by Nazi rule in the years after 1933 chose the military career because it seemed to offer the only decent atmosphere uninfluenced by the Party. The army, mentally against the Party, seemed to exist outside and without the Party as though it were a power of its own. It was another error of conscience; eventually, with all the independent generals in the old tradition eliminated, the consequences appeared as moral decay of the German officer in all positions of leadership—notwithstanding the many likable and even noble soldierly personalities who had sought salvation in vain, misled by a betraying conscience.

The very fact that honest consciousness and good-will were our initial guides is bound to deepen our later disillusionment and disappointment in ourselves. It leads us to question even our best faith; for we are responsible for our delusions—for every delusion to which we succumb.

Awakening and self-analysis of this delusion are indispensable. They turn idealistic youths into upright, morally reliable, politically lucid German men acquiescing in their lot as now cast.

(c) By partial approval of National-Socialism, by *straddling* and occasional *inner assimilation* and accommodation, moral guilt was incurred without any of the tragic aspects of the previous types.

The argument that there was some good to it, after all—this readiness to a supposedly unbiased appraisal—was widespread among us. Yet the truth could be only a radical "either-or": if I recognize the principle as evil, everything is evil and any seemingly good consequences are not what they seem to be. It was this erring objectiveness, ready to grant something good in National-Socialism, which estranged close friends so they could no longer talk frankly. The same man who had just lamented the failure of a martyr to appear and sacrifice himself for the old freedom and against injustice was apt to praise the abolition of unemployment (by means of armament and fraudulent financial policies), apt to hail the absorption of Austria in 1938 as the fulfillment of the old ideal of a united Reich, apt to cast doubts on Dutch neutrality in 1940 and to justify Hitler's attack, and apt, above all, to rejoice in the victories.

(d) Many engaged in convenient *self-deception*. In due time they were going to change this evil government. The Party would disappear again—with the Fuehrer's death at the latest. For the present one had to belong, to right things from within. The following conversations were typical:

An officer speaks: "After the war we'll finish National-Socialism on the very basis of our victory; but now we must stick together and lead Germany to that victory—when the house burns down you pour water and don't stop to ask what caused the fire."—Answer: "After victory you'll be discharged and glad to go home. The SS alone will stay armed, and the reign of terror will grow into a slave state. No individual human life will be possible; pyramids will rise; highways and towns will be built and changed at the Fuehrer's whim. A giant arms machine will be developed for the final conquest of the world."

A professor speaks: "We are the Fronde within the Party. We dare frank discussion. We achieve spiritual realizations. We shall slowly turn all of it back into the old German spirituality."—Answer: "You are deceiving yourselves. Allowed a fool's freedom, on condition of instant obedience, you shut up and give in. Your fight is a mirage, desired by the leaders. You only help to entomb the German spirit."

Many intellectuals went along in 1933, sought leading positions and publicly upheld the ideology of the new power, only to become resentful later when they personally were shunted aside. These—although mostly continuing positive until about 1942, when the course of the war made an unfavorable outcome certain and sent them into the oppositionist ranks—now feel that they suffered under the Nazis and are therefore called for what follows. They regard themselves as anti-Nazis. In all these years, according to their self-proclaimed ideology, these intellectual Nazis were frankly speaking truth in spiritual matters, guarding the tradition of the German spirit, preventing destructions, doing good in individual cases.

Many of these may be guilty of persisting in a mentality which, while not identical with Party tenets and even disguised as metamorphosis and opposition, still clings in fact to the mental attitude of National-Socialism and fails to clear itself. Through this mentality they may be actually akin to National-Socialism's inhuman, dictatorial, unexistentially nihilistic essence. If a mature person in 1933 had the certainty of inner conviction—due not merely to political error but to a sense of existence heightened by National-Socialism—he will be purified only by a transmutation which may have to be more thorough than any other. Whoever behaved like that in 1933 would remain inwardly brittle otherwise, and inclined to further fanaticism. Whoever took part in the race mania, whoever had delusions of a revival based on fraud, whoever winked at the crimes then already committed is not merely liable but must renew himself morally. Whether and how he can do it is up to him alone, and scarcely open to any outside scrutiny.

(e) There is a difference between *activity* and *passivity*. The political performers and executors, the leaders and the propagandists are guilty. If they did not become criminals, they still have, by their activity, incurred a positively determinable guilt.

But each one of us is guilty insofar as he remained inactive. The guilt of passivity is different. Impotence excuses; no moral law demands a spectacular death. Plato already deemed it a matter of course to go into hiding in desperate times of calamity, and to survive. But passivity knows itself morally guilty of every failure, every neglect to act whenever possible, to shield the imperiled, to relieve wrong, to countervail. Impotent submission always left a margin of activity which, though not without risk, could still be cautiously effective. Its anxious omission weighs upon the individual as moral guilt. Blindness for the misfortune of others, lack of imagination of the heart, inner indifference toward the witnessed evil—that is moral guilt.

(f) The moral guilt of outward compliance, of *running with the pack*, is shared to some extent by a great many of us. To maintain his existence, to keep his job, to protect his chances a man would join the Party and carry out other nominal acts of conformism.

Nobody will find an absolute excuse for doing so—notably in view of the many Germans who, in fact, did not conform, and bore the disadvantages.

Yet we must remember what the situation looked like in, say, 1936 or '37. The Party was the state. Conditions seemed incalculably permanent. Nothing short of a war could upset the régime. All the powers were appeasing Hitler. All wanted peace. A German who did not want to be out of everything, lose his profession, injure his business, was obliged to go along—the younger ones in particular. Now, membership in the Party or its professional organizations was no longer a political act; rather, it was a favor granted by the state which allowed the individual to join. A "badge" was needed, an external token without inner assent. A man asked to join in those days could hardly refuse. It is decisive for the meaning of compliance in what connection and from what motives he acquired his membership in the Party; each year and every situation has its own mitigating and aggravating circumstances, to be distinguished only in each individual case.

(70)

Morality is always influenced by mundane purposes. I may be morally bound to risk my life, if a realization is at stake; but there is no moral obligation to sacrifice one's life in the sure knowledge that nothing will have been gained. Morally we have a duty to dare, not a duty to choose certain doom. Morally, in either case, we rather have the contrary duty, not to do what cannot serve the mundane purpose but to save ourselves for realizations in the world.

But there is within us a guilt consciousness which springs from another source. Metaphysical guilt is the lack of absolute solidarity with the human being as such—an indelible claim beyond morally meaningful duty. This solidarity is violated by my presence at a wrong or a crime. It is not enough that I cautiously risk my life to prevent it; if it happens, and if I was there, and if I survive where the other is killed, I know from a voice within myself: I am guilty of being still alive.

I quote from an address* I gave in August 1945: "We ourselves have changed since 1933. It was possible for us to seek death in humiliation—in 1933 when the Constitution was torn up, the dictatorship established in sham legality and all resistance swept away in the intoxication of a large part of our people. We could seek death when the crimes of the régime became publicly apparent on June 30, 1934, or with the lootings, deportations and murders of our Jewish friends and fellow-citizens in 1938, when to our ineradicable

---

* Reprinted in *Wandlung*, Vol. I, No. 1, 1945.

shame and disgrace the synagogues, houses of God, went up in flames throughout Germany. We could seek death when from the start of the war the régime acted against the words of Kant, our greatest philosopher, who called it a premise of international law that nothing must occur in war which would make a later reconcilement of the belligerents impossible. Thousands in Germany sought, or at least found death in battling the régime, most of them anonymously. We survivors did not seek it. We did not go into the streets when our Jewish friends were led away; we did not scream until we too were destroyed. We preferred to stay alive, on the feeble, if logical, ground that our death could not have helped anyone. We are guilty of being alive. We know before God which deeply humiliates us. What happened to us in these twelve years is like a transmutation of our being."

In November 1938, when the synagogues burned and Jews were deported for the first time, the guilt incurred was chiefly moral and political. In either sense, the guilty were those still in power. The generals stood by. In every town the commander could act against crime, for the soldier is there to protect all, if crime occurs on such a scale that the police cannot or fail to stop it. They did nothing. At that moment they forsook the once glorious ethical tradition of the German Army. It was not their business. They had dissociated themselves from the soul of the German people, in favor of an absolute military machine that was a law unto itself and took orders.

True, among our people many were outraged and many deeply moved by a horror containing a presentiment of coming calamity. But even more went right on with their activities, undisturbed in their social life and amusements, as if nothing had happened. That is moral guilt.

But the ones who in utter impotence, outraged and despairing, were unable to prevent the crimes took another step in their metamorphosis by a growing consciousness of metaphysical guilt.

RECAPITULATION

Consequences of Guilt

If everything said before was not wholly unfounded, there can be no doubt that we Germans, every one of us, are guilty in some way. Hence there occur the consequences of guilt.

(1) All Germans without exception share in the political liability. All must cooperate in making amends to be brought into legal form. All must jointly suffer the effects of the acts of the victors, of their decisions, of their disunity. We are unable here to exert any influence as a factor of power.

Only by striving constantly for a sensible presentation of the facts, opportunities and dangers can we—unless everyone already knows what we say—collaborate on the premises of the decisions. In the proper form, and with reason, we may appeal to the victors.

(2) Not every German—indeed only a very small minority of Germans—will be punished for crimes. Another minority has to atone for National-Socialist activities. All may defend themselves. They will be judged by the courts of the victors, or by German courts established by the victors.

(3) Probably every German—though in greatly diverse

forms—will have reasons morally to analyze himself. Here, however, he need not recognize any authority other than his own conscience.

(4) And probably every German capable of understanding will transform his approach to the world and himself in the metaphysical experiences of such a disaster. How that happens none can prescribe, and none anticipate. It is a matter of individual solitude. What comes out of it has to create the essential basis of what will in future be the German soul.

Such distinctions can be speciously used to get rid of the whole guilt question, for instance like this:

Political liability—all right, but it curtails only my material possibilities; I myself, my inner self is not affected by that at all.

Criminal guilt—that affects just a few, not me; it does not concern me.

Moral guilt—I hear that my conscience alone has jurisdiction, others have no right to accuse me. Well, my conscience is not going to be too hard on me. It wasn't really so bad; let's forget about it, and make a fresh start.

Metaphysical guilt—of that, finally, I was expressly told that none can charge it to another. I am supposed to perceive that in a transmutation. That's a crazy idea of some philosopher. There is no such thing. And if there were, I wouldn't notice it. That I needn't bother with.

Our dissection of the guilt concepts can be turned into a trick, for getting rid of guilt. The distinctions are in the foreground. They can hide the source and the unity. Distinctions enable us to spirit away what does not suit us.

Having separated the elements of guilt, we return in the end to the question of collective guilt.

Though correct and meaningful everywhere, the separation carries with it the indicated temptation—as though by such distinctions we had dodged the charges and eased our burden. Something has been lost in the process—something which in collective guilt is always audible in spite of everything. For all the crudeness of collective thinking and collective condemnation we feel that we belong together.

In the end, of course, the true collective is the solidarity of all men before God. Somewhere, everyone may free himself from the bonds of state or people or group and break through to the invisible solidarity of men—as men of goodwill and as men sharing the common guilt of being human.

But historically we remain bound to the closer, narrower communities, and we should lose the ground under our feet without them.

POLITICAL LIABILITY AND COLLECTIVE GUILT

First to restate the fact that all over the world collective concepts largely guide the judgment and feelings of men. This is undeniable. In the world today the German—whatever the German may be—is regarded as something one would rather not have to do with. German Jews abroad are undesirable as Germans; they are essentially deemed Germans, not Jews. In this collective way of thought political liability is simultaneously justified as punishment of moral guilt.

Historically such collective thought is not infrequent; the barbarism of war has seized whole populations and delivered them to pillage, rape and sale into slavery. And on top of it comes moral annihilation of the unfortunates in the judgment of the victor. They shall not only submit but confess and do penance. Whoever is German, whether Christian or Jew, is evil in spirit.

This fact of a widespread, though not universal, world opinion keeps challenging us, not only to defend ourselves with our simple distinction of political liability and moral guilt but to examine what truth may possibly lie in collective thinking. We do not drop the distinction, but we have to narrow it by saying that the conduct which made us liable rests on a sum of political conditions whose nature is moral, as it were, because they help to determine individual morality. The individual cannot wholly detach himself from these conditions, for—consciously or unconsciously—he lives as a link in their chain and cannot escape from their influence even if he was in opposition. There is a sort of collective moral guilt in a people's way of life which I share as an individual, and from which grow political realities.

For political conditions are inseparable from a people's whole way of life. There is no absolute division of politics and human existence as long as man is still realizing an existence rather than perishing in eremitical seclusion.

By political conditions the Swiss, the Dutch have been formed, and all of us in Germany have been brought up for ages—we to obey, to feel dynastically, to be indifferent and irresponsible toward political reality—and these conditions are part of us even if we oppose them.

The way of life effects political events, and the resulting political conditions in turn place their imprint on the way of life. This is why there can be no radical separation of moral and political guilt. This is why every enlightenment of our political consciousness proportionately burdens our conscience. Political liberty has its moral aspects.

Thus, actual political liability is augmented by knowledge and then by a different self-esteem. That in fact all the people pay for all the acts of their government—*quidquid delirant reges plectuntur Achivi*—is a mere empirical fact; that they know themselves liable is the first indication of their dawning political liberty. It is to the extent of the existence and recognition of this knowledge that freedom is real, not a mere outward claim put forth by unfree men.

The inner political unfreedom has the opposite feeling. It obeys on the one hand, and feels not guilty on the other. The feeling of guilt, which makes us accept liability, is the beginning of the inner upheaval which seeks to realize political liberty.

The contrast of the free and the unfree mental attitude appears, for instance, in the two concepts of a statesman. The question has been raised whether nations are to blame for the leaders they put up with—for example, France for Napoleon. The idea is that the vast majority did go along and desired the power and the glory which Napoleon procured. In this view Napoleon was possible only because the French would have him; his greatness was the precision with which he understood what the mass of the people expected, what they wanted to hear, what illusions they wanted, what material realities they wanted. Could Lenz have been right in saying, "The state was born which suited the genius of France"? A part, a situation, yes—but not the genius of a nation as such! Who can define a national genius? The same genius has spawned very different realities.

One might think that, as a man must answer for his choice of the beloved to whom marriage binds him in a lifelong community of fate, a people answers for whomever it meekly obeys. Error is culpable; there is no escape from its consequences.

Precisely this, however, would be the wrong approach. The unconditional attachment to one person which is possible and proper in a marriage is pernicious on principle in a state. The loyalty of followers is a non-political relationship limited to narrow circles and primitive circumstances. In a free state all men are subject to control and change.

Hence there is twofold guilt—first, in the unconditional political surrender to a leader as such, and second, in the kind of leader submitted to. The atmosphere of submission is a sort of collective guilt.

All the restrictions concerning our liberation from moral guilt—in favor of mere political liability—do not affect what we established at the beginning and shall now restate:

We are politically responsible for our régime, for the acts of the regime, for the start of the war in this world-historical situation, and for the kind of leaders we allowed to rise among us. For that we answer to the victors, with our labor and with our working faculties, and must make such amends as are exacted from the vanquished.

In addition there is our moral guilt. Although this always burdens only the individual who must get along with himself, there still is a sort of collective morality contained in the ways of life and feeling, from which no individual can altogether escape and which have political significance as well. Here is the key to self-improvement; its use is up to us.

INDIVIDUAL AWARENESS OF COLLECTIVE GUILT

We feel something like a co-responsibility for the acts of members of our families. This co-responsibility cannot be objectivized. We should reject any manner of tribal liability. And yet, because of our consanguinity we are inclined to feel concerned whenever wrong is done by someone in the family —and also inclined, therefore, depending on the type and circumstances of the wrong and its victims, to make it up to them even if we are not morally and legally accountable.

Thus the German—that is, the German-speaking individual—feels concerned by everything growing from German roots. It is not the liability of a national but the concern of one who shares the life of the German spirit and soul— who is of one tongue, one stock, one fate with all the others—which here comes to cause, not as tangible guilt, but somehow analogous to co-responsibility.

We further feel that we not only share in what is done at present—thus being co-responsible for the deeds of our contemporaries—but in the links of tradition. We have to bear the guilt of our fathers. That the spiritual conditions of German life provided an opportunity for such a régime is a fact for which all of us are co-responsible. Of course this does not mean that we must acknowledge "the world of

(79)

German ideas" or "German thought of the past" in general as the sources of the National-Socialist misdeeds. But it does mean that our national tradition contains something, mighty and threatening, which is our moral ruin.

We feel ourselves not only as individuals but as Germans. Every one, in his real being, is the German people. Who does not remember moments in his life when he said to himself, in opposition and in despair of his nation, "I am Germany"—or, in jubilant harmony with it, "I, too, am Germany!" The German character has no other form than these individuals. Hence the demands of transmutation, of rebirth, of rejection of evil are made of the nation in the form of demands from each individual.

Because in my innermost soul I cannot help feeling collectively, being German is to me—is to everyone—not a condition but a task. This is altogether different from making the nation absolute. I am a human being first of all; in particular I am a Frisian, a professor, a German, linked closely enough for a fusion of souls with other collective groups, and more or less closely with all groups I have come in touch with. For moments this proximity enables me to feel almost like a Jew or Dutchman or Englishman. Throughout it, however, the fact of my being German—that is, essentially, of life in the mother tongue—is so emphatic that in a way which is rationally not conceivable, which is even rationally refutable, I feel co-responsible for what Germans do and have done.

I feel closer to those Germans who feel likewise—without becoming melodramatic about it—and farther from the ones whose soul seems to deny this link. And this proximity means, above all, a common inspiring task—of not being German as we happen to be, but becoming German as we are not yet but ought to be, and as we hear it in the call of our ancestors rather than in the history of national idols.

By our feeling of collective guilt we feel the entire task of renewing human existence from its origin—the task which is given to all men on earth but which appears more urgently, more perceptibly, as decisively as all existence, when its own guilt brings a people face to face with nothingness.

As a philosopher I now seem to have strayed completely into the realm of feeling and to have abandoned conception. Indeed language fails at this point, and only negatively we may recall that all our distinctions—notwithstanding the fact that we hold them to be true and are by no means rescinding them—must not become resting places. We must not use them to let matters drop and free ourselves from the pressure under which we continue on our path, and which is to ripen what we hold most precious, the eternal essence of our soul.

Possible Excuses

Both we ourselves and those who wish us well are ready with ideas to alleviate our guilt. There can be no question of nullifying such guilt as we, distinguishing and reassembling, have developed here; but there are points of view which, by suggesting a more lenient judgment, simultaneously sharpen and characterize the type of guilt referred to at each time.

TERRORISM

Germany under the Nazi régime was a prison. The guilt of getting into it is political guilt. Once the gates were shut, however, a prison break from within was no longer possible. Any discussion of what responsibility and guilt of the imprisoned remained and arose thereafter must consider the question what they could do at all.

To hold the inmates of a prison collectively responsible for outrages committed by the prison staff is clearly unjust.

It has been said that the millions—the millions of workers and the millions of soldiers—should have resisted. Since they did not, since they worked and fought for the war, they are considered guilty.

(82)

We may say in rebuttal that the 15,000,000 foreign workers worked just as well for the war as did the German workers. There is no evidence that more sabotage acts were committed by them. Only in the final weeks, with the collapse already under way, the foreign workers seem to have become active on a larger scale.

Large-scale actions are impossible without organization and leadership. To ask a people to rise even against a terrorist state is to ask the impossible. Such rebellion can only be a scattered, disconnected occurrence, generally anonymous, subsequently unknown—a quiet submersion in death. Only a few exceptions were publicized by special circumstances, and these only orally and in narrow limits (as the heroism of the two students, Scholls, and of Professor Huber in Munich).

This being so, we marvel at some accusations. Franz Werfel, in an unmerciful indictment of the whole German people written shortly after the collapse of Hitler Germany, says that "only the one Niemoeller resisted." In the same article he mentions the hundreds of thousands who were killed in the concentration camps—why? Surely because they resisted, although for the most part only by word. The ineffective disappearance of these anonymous martyrs underlines the impossibility. After all, concentration camps were a purely domestic affair until 1939, and even after that they were filled largely with Germans. In every month of 1944 the number of political arrests exceeded 4,000. The fact that there were concentration camps until the very end proves that there was opposition in the country.

At times we seem to hear a pharisaical note in the charges,

from those who perilously made their escape but finally—measured by suffering and death in concentration camps, and by the fear in Germany—lived abroad without terrorist compulsion, though with the sorrows of exile, and now claim credit for their emigration as such. This note we deem ourselves entitled to reject, without anger.

Some righteous voices have indeed been raised precisely in discernment of the terror apparatus and its consequences. Thus Dwight Macdonald wrote in the magazine *Politics* in March 1945: "The peak of terror and of guilt enforced by terror was achieved with the alternative, Kill or be killed," and he added that many commanders assigned to executions and murders refused to take part in the cruelties and were shot.

Thus Hannah Arendt wrote about the participation and the complicity of the German people in the crimes of the Fuehrer as the result of organized terror. Family men, simple jobholders, whom nobody would ever have suspected of being capable of murder and who always had done their duty, now obeyed the orders to kill people and to commit other atrocities in the concentration camps with the same sense of duty.*

GUILT WITHIN HISTORY

We distinguish between cause and guilt. An exposition showing why things happened as they did, and why indeed they

---

* Hannah Arendt's moving, soberly factual article, "Organized Guilt," *Jewish Frontier*, January, 1945.

could not but so happen, is automatically considered an excuse. A cause is blind and involuntary. Guilt is seeing and free.

We usually deal in like fashion with political events. The causal connection of history seems to relieve a people of responsibility. Hence their satisfaction if, in adversity, effective causes seem to make inevitability plausible.

Many tend to accept and stress their responsibility when they talk of their present actions whose arbitrariness they would like to see released from restraints, conditions and obligations. In case of failure, on the other hand, they tend to decline responsibility and plead allegedly inescapable necessities. Responsibility had been a talking point, not an experience.

All through these years, accordingly, one could hear that if Germany won the war the victory and the credit would be the Party's—while if Germany lost, the losers and the guilty would be the German people.

But actually, in the causal connections of history, cause and responsibility are indivisible wherever human activity is at work. As soon as decisions and actions play a part in events, every cause is at the same time either credit or guilt.

Even those happenings which are independent of will and decision still are human tasks. The effects of natural causes depend also on how man takes them, how he handles them, what he makes out of them. Cognition of history, therefore, is never such as to apprehend its course as flatly necessary. This cognition can never make certain predictions (as possible, for instance, in astronomy), nor can it retrospectively perceive an inevitability of general events and individual actions. In either case it sees the scope of possibilities, only more richly and concretely in the case of the past.

In turn, this cognition, historic-sociological insight and the resulting picture of history, affects events and is to this extent a matter of responsibility.

Chiefly named as premises independent of freedom—and thus of guilt and responsibility—are the conditions of geography and the world-historical situation.

Geographical Conditions

Germany has open borders all around. To maintain itself as a nation, it must be militarily strong at all times. Periods of weakness have made it a prey to aggression from the West, East and North, finally even from the South (Turks). Because of its geographical situation Germany never knew the peace of an unmenaced existence, as England knew it and, even more so, America. England could afford to pay for its magnificent domestic evolution in decades of impotence in foreign politics and military weakness. It was by no means conquered for that reason; its last invasion took place in 1066. A country such as Germany, uncemented by natural frontiers, was forced to develop military states to keep its nationhood alive at all. This function was long performed by Austria, later by Prussia.

The peculiarity and military style of each state would mark the rest of Germany and yet would always be felt also as alien. It took an effort to gloss over the fact that Germany either had to be ruled by something which, though German, was alien to the rest, or would in the impotence of a scattered whole be left at the mercy of foreign nations.

Thus Germany had no lasting center, only transient centers of gravity, with the result that none could be felt and recognized as its own by more than a part of Germany.

Nor, indeed, was there a spiritual center, a common meeting ground for all Germans. Even our classic literature and philosophy had not yet become the property of our whole people. They belonged to a small, educated stratum, though one extending as far as German was spoken, beyond the borders of the German state. And of unanimity in acknowledging greatness there is no trace here, either.

We might say that the geographical situation not only compelled German militarism with its consequences—the prevalence of authority-worship and servility, the lack of libertarianism and a democratic spirit—but also made a necessarily transient phenomenon of every organized state. To last awhile, any state required favorable circumstances and superior, unusually prudent statesmen, while a single irresponsible political leader could permanently ruin Germany and the state.

Yet however true this basic trait of our reflections may be, it is important for us not to interpret it as absolute necessity. In what direction the military develop, whether or not wise leaders appear—these things are in no way to be blamed on the geographical situation.

In a similar situation, for example, the political energy, solidarity and prudence of the Romans produced quite different results—a united Italy and later a world empire, although one which in the end crushed liberty, too. The study of republican Rome is of great interest as showing how a military development and imperialism led a democratic people to the loss of liberty and to dictatorship.

If geographical conditions leave a margin of freedom, the decisive factor beyond guilt and responsibility is generally said to be the "natural" national character. This, however, is a refuge of ignorance and an instrument of false evaluations—whether appreciative or depreciative.

There probably is something in the natural foundation of our vital existence which has effects extending to the peak of our spirituality—but we may say that our knowledge of it is virtually nil. The intuition of direct impression—as evident as it is deceptive, as compelling for the moment as it is unreliable at length—has not been raised to the level of real knowledge by any racial theory.

In fact, we always describe national character in terms of arbitrarily selected historical phenomena. Yet these in turn have always been caused by events, and by conditions marked by events. At every time they are one group of phenomena, appearing only as one of many types. Other situations might bring entirely different, otherwise hidden character traits to the fore. A distinct natural character complete with talents may very well exist, but we simply do not know it.

We must not shift our responsibility to anything like that. As men we must know ourselves free for all possibilities.

THE WORLD-HISTORICAL SITUATION

The position of Germany in the world, world events at large, the others' conduct toward Germany—all this is the more important for Germany since its defenseless central geographical location exposes it more than other countries to influences from outside. This is why Ranke's assertion of the primacy of foreign over domestic politics is true of Germany but not of history in general.

The political connections of the last half-century—especially of the events and modes of conduct since 1918, since the Allies' first victory over Germany—will not be presented here, although they were certainly not immaterial to the developments which became possible in Germany. I shall glance only at an inner, spiritual world phenomenon. Perhaps—but who could dare assert real cognition here?—we may say this:

What broke out in Germany was under way in the entire Western world as a crisis of faith, of the spirit.

This does not diminish our guilt—for it was here in Germany that the outbreak occurred, not somewhere else—but it does free us from absolute isolation. It makes us instructive for the others. It concerns all.

This world-historical crisis is not simply defined. The declining effectiveness of the Christian and Biblical faith; the lack of faith seeking a substitute; the social upheaval, due to technology and production methods, which in the nature of things leads irresistibly to socialist orders in which the masses of the population, that is everyone, comes to his human right—these upheavals are under way. Everywhere the situation is more or less so as to make men call for a change. In such a case the ones who are hardest hit, most deeply aware of their lack of contentment, incline to hasty, untimely, deceptive, fraudulent solutions.

In a development which has seized the world, Germany danced such a fraudulent solo to its doom.

THE OTHERS' GUILT

Whoever has not yet found himself guilty in spontaneous self-analysis will tend to accuse his accusers. For instance, he may ask whether they are better than the ones they censure, or whether they do not share the guilt of events, because of acts which could not but promote such possibilities.

Among us Germans the tendency to hit back at present indicates that we have not yet understood ourselves. For the first thing each of us needs in disaster is clarity about himself. The foundation of our new life must come from the origin of our being and can only be achieved in unreserved self-analysis.

This does not mean, however, that we must close our eyes to the facts and to truth in regarding the other nations, to which Germany owes its final liberation from the Hitler yoke and to whose decision our future is entrusted.

We must and we may elucidate to ourselves how the others' conduct has made our situation more difficult, on the domestic and on the foreign scene. For their past and future actions come from the world in which we, entirely dependent on it, are to find our way. We must shun illusions and come to a correct overall evaluation. We must yield neither to blind hostility nor to blind hope.

If we use the words, "guilt of the others," it may mislead us. If they, by their conduct, made events possible, this is political guilt. But in discussing it we must never for a moment forget that this guilt is on another level than the crimes of Hitler.

Two points seem essential: the political acts of the victorious powers since 1918, and their inactivity while Hitler Germany was organizing itself.

(1) England, France and America were the victorious powers of 1918. The course of world history was in their hands, not in those of the vanquished. The victor's responsibility is his alone, to accept or to evade. If he evades it, his historical guilt is plain.

The victor cannot be entitled simply to withdraw to his own narrower sphere, there to be left alone and merely watch what happens elsewhere in the world. If an event threatens dire consequences, he has the power to prevent it. To have this power and fail to use it is political guilt. To be content with paper protests is evasion of responsibility. This inaction is one charge that may be brought against the victorious powers—although, of course, it does not free us from any guilt.

In discussing this further, one may point to the peace treaty of Versailles and its consequences, and then to the policy of letting Germany slide into the conditions which produced National-Socialism. Next, one may bring up the toleration of the Japanese invasion of Manchuria—the first act of violence which, if successful, was bound to be copied —and the toleration of Mussolini's act of violence, the Ethiopian campaign of 1935. One may deplore the policy of England which in Geneva defeated Mussolini through the League of Nations and then let its resolutions stay on paper, lacking the will and the strength required to destroy

Mussolini in fact, but also lacking the clear radicality to steer an opposite course, to join him and, while slowly changing his regime, stand with him against Hitler to insure peace. For Mussolini then was ready to side with the Western powers against Germany; as late as 1934 he mobilized his forces and delivered a threatening, since forgotten speech as Hitler wanted to march into Austria. The result of these half-measures was the alliance of Mussolini and Hitler.

However, it must be pointed out here that no one knows what further consequences different decisions might have had. And above all: British policy also has moral aspects—a fact which National-Socialism actually included in its calculations, as British weakness. The British cannot unrestrainedly make any decision that is politically effective. They want peace. They want to utilize every chance of preserving it before they take extreme measures. They are not ready to go to war until war is obviously inescapable.

(2) There is a solidarity not only among fellow-citizens but also among Europeans and among mankind. The responsibility of the inactive bystander ranges from the mutual one of fellow-citizens to one that is universally human.

Rightly or wrongly, once the gates had shut on our German prison we were hoping for European solidarity.

As yet we had no idea of the last horrible consequences and crimes. But we saw the utter loss of liberty. We knew that now the arbitrary tyranny of those in power was given free rein. We saw injustice, saw outcasts, though all of it was still harmless in comparison with later years. We knew about concentration camps, though ignorant still of the cruelties going on there.

Certainly all of us in Germany were jointly guilty of getting into this political situation, of losing our freedom and having to live under the despotism of uncivilized brutes. But at the same time we could say in extenuation that we had been victimized by a combination of veiled illegalities and open violence. As in a state the victim of crime is accorded his rights by virtue of the state order, we were hopeful that a European order would not permit such crimes on the part of a state.

I shall never forget a talk in May 1933, in my home, with a friend who later emigrated and now lives in America. Longingly we weighed the chances of quick action by the Western powers: "If they wait another year, Hitler will have won; Germany, perhaps all Europe, will be lost. . . ."

It was in this state of mind, touched in the marrow of our bones and therefore clairvoyant in some respects and blind in others, that we felt increasing dismay at events like the following:

In the early summer of 1933 the Vatican signed a concordat with Hitler. Papen handled the negotiations. It was the first great indorsement of the Nazi régime, a tremendous prestige gain for Hitler. It seemed impossible, at first, but it was a fact. It made us shudder.

All nations recognized the Hitler régime. Admiring voices were heard.

In 1936 the world flocked to Berlin for the Olympic Games. Grimly we watched the appearance of every foreigner, unable to suppress a painful feeling that he was deserting us. But they did not know any better than many Germans.

In 1936 Hitler occupied the Rhineland. France let it happen.

In 1938 the London *Times* published an open letter from Churchill to Hitler, including sentences like the following (I remember it myself but quote from Roepke): "Were England to suffer a national disaster comparable to that of Germany in 1918, I should pray God to send us a man of your strength of mind and will. . . ."

In 1935, through Ribbentrop, England signed a naval pact with Hitler. This was what it meant to us: The British abandon the German people for the sake of peace with Hitler. They care nothing about us. They have not yet accepted European responsibilities. They not only stand by, as evil grows here—they meet it halfway. They allow a terrorist military state to engulf the Germans. For all the strictures of their press they do not act. We in Germany are powerless, but they might still—today, perhaps, still without excessive sacrifices—restore freedom among us. They are not doing it. The consequences will affect them, too, and exact vastly greater sacrifices.

In 1939 Russia made its pact with Hitler and thus, at the last moment, put Hitler in position to make war. And when war came, all neutral countries stood aside. The world failed utterly to join hands for one common effort, for the quick extinction of the devilry.

In Roepke's book on Germany, published in Switzerland, the overall situation of the years between 1933 and 1939 is characterized as follows:

"The present world catastrophe is the gigantic price the world must pay for playing deaf to all the warning signals which ever more shrilly, from 1930 until 1939, portended the hell to be loosed by the satanic forces of National-Socialism—first upon Germany, and then on the rest of the world. The terrors of this war correspond exactly to those which the world permitted to happen in Germany while maintaining normal relations with the National-Socialists and joining them at international festivals and conventions.

"Everyone should realize by now that the Germans were the first victims of the barbaric invasion which swamped them from below, that they were the first to succumb to terror and mass hypnosis, and that whatever had to be suffered later in occupied countries was first inflicted on the Germans themselves—including the worst of fates: to be forced or tricked into serving as tools of further conquest and oppression."

The charge that we, under terrorism, stood by inactively while the crimes were committed and the régime was consolidated is true. We have the right to recall that the others, not under terrorism, also remained inactive—that they let pass, if they did not unwittingly foster, events which, as occurring in another country, they did not regard as their concern.

Shall we admit that we alone are guilty?

Yes—if the question is who started the war; who initiated the terrorist organization of all forces for the sole purpose of war; who, as a nation, betrayed and sacrificed its own essence; and furthermore, who committed peculiar, unparalleled atrocities. Dwight Macdonald says that all sides committed many atrocities of war but that some things were peculiarly German: a paranoiac hatred without political sense; a fiendishness of agonies inflicted rationally with all means of modern science and technology, beyond all medieval torture tools. Yet there the guilty were a few Germans, a small group (plus an indefinite number of others capable of cooperating under orders). German anti-Semitism was not at any time a popular movement. The population failed to cooperate in the German pogroms; there were no spontaneous acts of cruelty against Jews. The mass of the people, if it did not feebly express its resentment, was silent and withdrew.

Shall we admit that we alone are guilty?

No—if we as a whole, as a people, as a permanent species, are turned into *the* evil people, the guilty people as such. Against this world opinion we can point to facts.

Yet all such discussions jeopardize our inner attitude unless we constantly remember what shall now be repeated once more:

(1) Any guilt which can be placed on the others, and which they place on themselves, is never that of the crimes of Hitler Germany. They merely let things drift at the time, took half-measures and erred in their political judgment.

That in the later course of the war our enemies also had prison camps as concentration camps and engaged in types of warfare previously started by Germany is secondary. Here we are not discussing events since the armistice, nor what Germany suffered and keeps on suffering after the surrender.

(2) The purpose of our discussion, even when we talk of a guilt of the others, is to penetrate the meaning of our own.

(3) In general, it may be correct that "the others are not better than we." But at this moment it is misapplied. For in these past twelve years the others, taken for all in all, were indeed better than we. A general truth must not serve to level out the particular, present truth of our own guilt.

GUILT OF ALL?

If we hear the imperfections in the political conduct of the powers explained as universal inevitabilities of politics, we may say in reply that this is the common guilt of mankind.

For us, the recapitulation of the others' actions does not have the significance of alleviating our guilt. Rather, it is justified by the anxiety which as human beings we share with all others for mankind—mankind as a whole, which not only has become conscious of its existence today but, due to the results of technology, has developed a trend toward a common order, which may succeed or fail.

The basic fact that all of us are human justifies this anxiety of ours about human existence as a whole. There is a passionate desire in our souls, to stay related or to re-establish relations with humanity as such.

How much easier we should breathe if, instead of being as human as we are, the victors were selfless world governors! With wisdom and foresight they would direct a propitious reconstruction including effective amends. Their lives and actions would be an example demonstrating the ideal of democratic conditions, and daily making us feel it as a convincing reality. United among themselves in reasonable, frank talk without mental reservations, they would quickly and sensibly decide all arising questions. No deception and no illusion would be possible, no silent concealment and no discrepancy between public and private utterances. Our people would receive a splendid education; we should achieve the liveliest nationwide development of our thinking and appropriate the most substantial tradition. We should be dealt with sternly but justly and kindly, even charitably, if the unfortunate and misguided showed only the slightest good-will.

But the others are human as we are. And they hold the future of mankind in their hands. Since we are human, all our existence and the possibilities of our being are bound up with their doings and with the results of their actions. So, to us, to sense what they want, think and do is like our own affair.

In this anxiety we ask ourselves: could the other nations' better luck be due in part to more favorable political destinies? Could they be making the same mistakes that we made, only so far without the fatal consequences which led to our undoing?

They would reject any warnings from us wicked wretches. They would fail to understand, perhaps, and might even find it presumptuous if Germans should worry over the course of history—which is their business, not that of the

Germans. And yet, we are oppressed by one nightmarish idea: if a dictatorship in Hitler's style should ever rise in America, all hope would be lost for ages. We in Germany could be freed from the outside. Once a dictatorship has been established, no liberation from within is possible. Should the Anglo-Saxon world be dictatorially conquered from within, as we were, there would no longer be an outside, nor a liberation. The freedom fought for and won by Western man over hundreds, thousands of years would be a thing of the past. The primitivity of despotism would reign again, but with all means of technology. True, man cannot be forever enslaved; but this comfort would then be a very distant one, on a plane with Plato's dictum that in the course of infinite time everything that is possible will here or there occur or recur as a reality. We see the feelings of moral superiority and we are frightened: he who feels absolutely safe from danger is already on the way to fall victim to it. The German fate could provide all others with experience. If only they would understand this experience! We are no inferior race. Everywhere people have similar qualities. Everywhere there are violent, criminal, vitally capable minorities apt to seize the reins if occasion offers, and to proceed with brutality.

We may well worry over the victors' self-certainty. For all decisive responsibility for the course of events will henceforth be theirs. It is up to them to prevent evil or conjure up new evil. Whatever guilt they might incur from now on would be as calamitous for us as for them. Now that the whole of mankind is at stake, their responsibility for their actions is intensified. Unless a break is made in the evil chain, the fate which overtook us will overtake the victors—and all of mankind with them. The myopia of human thinking—especially in the form of a world opinion pouring over everything at times like an irresistible tide—constitutes a huge danger. The instruments of God are not God on earth. To repay evil with evil—notably to the jailed, not merely the jailers—would make evil and bear new calamities.

In tracing our own guilt back to its source we come upon the human essence—which in its German form has fallen into a peculiar, terrible incurring of guilt but exists as a possibility in man as such.

Thus German guilt is sometimes called the guilt of all: the hidden evil everywhere is jointly guilty of the outbreak of evil in this German place.

It would, indeed, be an evasion and a false excuse if we Germans tried to exculpate ourselves by pointing to the guilt of being human. It is not relief but greater depth to which the idea can help us. The question of original sin must not become a way to dodge German guilt. Knowledge of original sin is not yet insight into German guilt. But neither must the religious confession of original sin serve as guise for a false German confession of collective guilt, with the one in dishonest haziness taking the place of the other.

We feel no desire to accuse the others; we do not want to infect them as it were, to drag them onto our path of doom. But at the distance and with the anxiey of those who stumbled onto it and now come to and reflect, we think:

(100)

if only the others might not walk in such ways—if only those among us who are of good-will might be able to rely on them.

Now a new period of history has begun. From now on, responsibility for whatever happens rests with the victorious powers.

Our Purification

The self-analysis of a people in historical reflection and the personal self-analysis of the individual are two different things. But the first can happen only by way of the second. What individuals accomplish jointly in communication may, if true, become the spreading consciousness of many and then is called national consciousness.

Again we must reject collective thinking, as fictitious thinking. Any real metamorphosis occurs through individuals —in the individual, in many individuals independent of or mutually inspiring one another.

We Germans, no matter how differently or even contrastingly, all ponder our guilt or guiltlessness. All of us do, National-Socialists and opponents of National-Socialism. By "we" I mean those with whom language, descent, situation, fate, give me a feeling of immediate solidarity. I do not mean to accuse anyone by saying, "We." If other Germans feel guiltless, that is up to them—except in the two points of the punishment of criminals for crimes and of the political liability of all for the acts of the Hitler state. Those feeling guiltless are not being assailed until they start assailing. If in considering themselves guiltless they call others guilty, we should, of course, always inquire into the substance of their charges but also into their right to make them here. If, however, continuing the National-Socialist type of thought, they call us un-German—if instead of meditating and listening to reason they blindly seek to destroy others by means of generalized judgments, they disrupt our solidarity and are unwilling to test and develop themselves by talking with each other. For their way of attack they are to be charged with violating human rights.

Among our population a natural insight, thoughtful and without pathos, is not rare. The following are samples of such simple utterances.

An eighty-year-old scholar: "I never wavered in these twelve years, and yet I was never satisfied with myself. Time and again I would ruminate whether the purely passive resistance to the Nazis might not be turned into action. But Hitler's organization was too diabolical."

A younger anti-Nazi: "After years of bowing to 'government by fear,' even though with gnashing teeth, we opponents of National-Socialism also need purification. Thus we dissociate ourselves from the pharisaism of those who think the mere absence of a Party badge makes them first-class people."

An official in the process of denazification: "If I let myself be pushed into the Party, if I lived in relative comfort, if I adapted myself to the Nazi state and to this extent benefited from it—even though in inner opposition—I have no decent right to complain if now I reap the disadvantages."

Our use of the word purification in the guilt question has a good sense. We have to purge ourselves of whatever

(103)

guilt each one finds in himself, as far as this is possible by restitution, by atonement, by inner renewal and metamorphosis. We shall come to that later.

First we shall glance at some of the tendencies which are tempting us to evade purification. Lured by false impulses and instincts, we not only leave the way that might cleanse us but add to confusion by unclean motivations.

Dodging Purification

Mutual Accusations

We Germans differ greatly in the kind and degree of our participation in, or resistance to, National-Socialism. Everyone must reflect on his own internal and external conduct, and seek his own peculiar rebirth in this German crisis.

Another great difference between individuals concerns the starting time of this inner metamorphosis—whether it began in 1933 or in 1934, after the murders of June 30; whether it happened from 1938 on, after the synagogue burnings, or not until the war, or not until the threatening defeat, or not until the collapse.

In these matters we Germans cannot be reduced to a common denominator. We must keep an open mind in approaching each other from essentially different starting points. The only common denominator may be our nationality which makes all jointly guilty and liable for having let 1933 come to pass without dying. This also unites the outer and the inner emigration.

Due to our great diversity, everybody can apparently

blame everybody else. This lasts as long as the individual really envisions only his own situation and that of people similar to him, and judges the situation of the others only in relation to himself. It is amazing to observe how we get really excited only when we are personally concerned, and how we see everything in the perspective of our special position. It takes a constant, conscious effort to escape from this perspective.

A recital of the recriminations current among the Germans of today would lead to endless discussions. Only some incidental examples from the present and the recent past are to be mentioned here. We may well falter at times, when our patience threatens to give out in talking with each other and we run up against brusque and callous rejection.

In the past years there were Germans who demanded martyrdom of us other Germans. We should not silently suffer what was going on, they told us; even if our action remained unsuccessful, it still would be like an ethical prop for the entire population, a visible symbol of suppressed forces. Thus I could hear myself rebuked from 1933 on, by friends, men and women.

Such demands were so harrowing because there was profound truth in them, yet a truth insultingly perverted by the manner of its presentation. What man, by himself, can experience before the transcendent, was dragged down to a level of moralizing, if not of sensationalism. Quietude and reverence were lost.

At present, a bad example of dodging into mutual accusation is given in many discussions between emigrants and others who stayed here—between the two groups we have come to describe as outer and inner emigration. Each has its ordeal. The emigrant has the world of a strange language to contend with, and homesickness as in the symbolic story of the German Jew in New York who had Hitler's picture on the wall of his room. Why? Because nothing short of this daily reminder of the horrors awaiting him here would let him master his longing for the homeland. The trials of the stay-at-home included being utterly forsaken, an outcast in his own country, in constant danger, alone in the hour of need, shunned by all save a few friends whom he endangered in turn, thus suffering anew. Yet if now one group accuses the other, we need but to ask ourselves how we feel about the inner condition and tone of voice of these accusers—whether we are happy that such people feel this way, whether they set an example, whether there is something of an uplift in them, of freedom, of love, which might encourage us. If not, then what they say is not true, either.

There is no growth of life in mutual accusation. Talking with each other actually ceases; it is a form of the severance of communication. And this in turn is always a symptom of untruth, and so an occasion for honest men to search unceasingly where untruth might be hiding. It hides wherever Germans presume to judge Germans morally and metaphysically; wherever the veiled will to compulsion reigns instead of the good-will to communication; wherever there is zeal to have the other admit guilt; wherever arrogance—"I am not incriminated"—looks down on the other; wherever the feeling of guiltlessness holds itself entitled to hold others guilty.

Our human disposition—in Europe, at least—is such as to make us equally sensitive to blame and quick to blame others. We do not want our toes stepped on, but in our moral judgment of others we get excited easily. This is the consequence of moralistic poisoning. There is generally nothing to which we are so sensitive as to any hint that we are considered guilty. Even if we are guilty we do not want to let ourselves be told. And if we let ourselves be told we still do not want to be told by everyone. The greater this sensitivity to blame, the greater, as a rule, is the inconsiderate readiness to blame others. The world, down to the petty circumstances of everyday life, teems with imputations of the authorship of some mischance.

Oddly, sensitivity to blame is very apt to rebound into an urge to confess. Such confessions of guilt—false, because still instinctive and lustful—have one unmistakable external trait: fed by the same will to power as their opposites in the same individual, they betray the confessor's wish to enhance his worth by his confession, to eclipse others. His confession of guilt wants to force others to confess. There is a touch of aggressiveness in such confessions. Moralism as a phenomenon of the will to power fosters both sensitivity to blame and confessions of guilt, both reproach and self-reproach, and psychologically it causes each of these to rebound into the other.

Hence, philosophically, the first thing required of anyone dealing with guilt questions is that he deal with himself, thereby extinguishing both sensitivity and the confession urge.

Today this generally human phenomenon—here described psychologically—is indissolubly interwoven with the gravity of our German question. We are threatened by the twin errors of self-abasing lamentation in confessions of guilt and of defiantly self-isolating pride.

The material concerns of the moment lead many astray. Confessing guilt strikes them as advantageous. Their eagerness to confess corresponds to the world's indignation at German moral turpitude. The powerful are met with flattery; one likes to say what they would like to hear. In addition, there is the baneful tendency to feel that confessing guilt makes us better than others. Humility cloaks an evil self-conceit. Self-disparagement contains an attack on others who refrain from it. The ignominy of such cheap self-accusations, the disgrace of supposedly helpful flattery, is obvious. At this point the power instincts of the mighty and the impotent fatally interlock.

Defiant pride is different. The moral attack of the others is the very reason for its stiffened obstinacy. It aims at self-respect in a supposed inner independence. But this is not to be gained if the decisive point remains obscure.

The decisive point is an eternal basic phenomenon, returned today in new form: he who in total defeat prefers life to death can only live in truthfulness—the only dignity left to him—if he decides upon this life in full realization of its meaning. What Hegel showed in his "Phenomenology," in the grandiose chapter on master and servant, is the necessity which human consciousness would like to obscure in order to evade it.

The decision to stay alive in impotence and servitude is an act of life-building sincerity. It results in a metamorphosis that modifies all values. Here—if the decision is made, if the consequences are accepted and toil and suffering embraced—lies the sublime potential of the human soul. In Hegel's exposition it is the servant rather than the master who bears the spiritual future—but not unless he honestly follows his hard road. Nothing is given. Nothing comes by itself. The errors of self-abasement and proud defiance can be avoided only if this prime decision is clear; purification serves to clarify both the decision and its consequences.

The presence of guilt, together with defeat, adds a psychological complication. Not only impotence but guilt must be accepted, and the transmutation which man would like to avoid must grow from both.

Proud defiance finds a multitude of points of view, of grandiloquences and edifying sentimentalities, to help itself to the delusion by which it can be maintained. For instance:

The meaning of the necessity to accept past events is changed. A wild inclination to "own up to our history" permits the concealed affirmation of evil, the discovery of good in evil, and its preservation in the soul as a proud fortress held against the victors. This perversion admits of sentences such as the following: "We must know that within us we still bear the primordial strength of will which created the past, and we must also stand by it and accept it into our existence. . . . We have been both and shall remain both . . . and we ourselves are never anything but our entire history

(109)

whose strength we bear within us." "Reverence" will force the new German generation to become like the previous one.

A defiance disguised as reverence is here confusing the historic soil—in which we are lovingly rooted—with the entirety of the realities of our common past. Far from loving all of those, we reject a good many as alien to our being.

In this affirming recognition of the evil as evil, queer emotional obscurities may admit of sentences such as the following: "We must become so brave and so great and so gentle that we can say, yes, even this horror was and will remain our reality, but we are strong enough to make it over within ourselves, for creative tasks. We know within us a fearful potentiality which once appeared in miserably erring forms. We love and esteem our whole historic past with a reverent affection transcending any single historic guilt. We bear this volcano within us, daring to know that it may blow us up, but convinced that only our ability to tame it will open the last expanse of our freedom and we realize, in the dangerous strength of such possibility, what in common with all others will be the human achievement of our spirit."

This is a tempting appeal—born of a bad, irrationalist philosophy—to avoid a decision and intrust ourselves to a process of existential levelling. "Taming" is not half enough. The "choice" is what matters. Failure to make the choice immediately revives the possibility of an evil defiance, bound to end up by saying, "Go and sin." The misapprehension in this appeal to reverence toward evil, even though it is negated, is that it could only lead to an illusive community.

A third manner of proud defiance may affirm all National-

Socialism as a matter of "philosophy of history"—in an esthetic view compounding obvious evil and disaster, which should be soberly considered, into an emotional fog of false magnificence:

"In the spring of 1932 a German philosopher prophesied that within ten years the world would be governed politically from two poles only, Moscow and Washington; that Germany, in between, would become irrelevant as a political-geographical conception, existing only as a spiritual power.

"German history—to which the defeat of 1918 had actually opened vistas of greater consolidation and even Great-German achievement—revolted against this prophesied and indeed impending tendency to simplify the world around two poles. Against this world tendency, German history contracted for an isolated, self-willed, titanic effort still to reach its own national goal.

"If that philosopher's prophecy was right in placing a time limit of only ten years on the beginning of Russo-American world rule, the precipitate pace, the haste and violence of the German countereffort was understandable. It was the pace of an inwardly meaningful and fascinating but historically belated revolt. In the past months we have seen this pace eventually outrun itself in pure, isolated raving. A philosopher lightly pronounces sentence: German history is past; the Moscow-Washington era is beginning. So greatly, longingly devised a history as the German one does not simply say, amen, to such academic resolutions. It flares up; in deeply excited resistance and attack, in a savage tumult of faith and hatred it plunges to its doom."

Thus, in the summer of 1945, a young man who has my

highest personal esteem wrote in a confusion of dismal feelings.

All this is indeed not purification but further entanglement. Thoughts like these—whether self-abasing or defiant—may for an instant evoke feelings as of delivery. You think you are back on your way, and actually you have only come closer to a dead end. It is the impurity of feelings which is here increased and simultaneously consolidated against the chance of a genuine metamorphosis.

All types of defiance feature an aggressive silence. I withdraw when reasons become irrefutable. I found my self-respect on silence as the last power left the powerless. I show my silence so as to hurt the powerful. I hide my silence so as to plan for a restoration, politically by seizing implements of power—laughable though these would be in the hands of men without access to the world's giant industries that produce the tools of destruction—and psychologically by a self-vindication admitting of no guilt. Fate decided against me; there was a senseless material superiority; my defeat was honorable; within myself I tend my loyalty and my heroism. But the way of such conduct merely augments the inner poison, in illusive thought and anticipating self-intoxication.

Dodging into Specialties Intrinsically Correct but Unessential to the Guilt Question

We are evading the guilt question if we deviate from essentials into intrinsically correct details—as if these were the whole—or if we persistently seek, and indeed find, fault with others.

In appropriate circumstances, a patient striving for common sense permits the submission of facts and connections to the victor. Now that we Germans are no longer active in the whole of history, we look upon what is and is not done as deciding our fate as well. Yet however correct this line of thought may be, it must not serve to replace or extinguish the guilt question.

The form of evasion most easily understood is the glance at our own woes. Help us, many think, but don't talk of atonement. Tremendous suffering excuses. We hear, for example:

"Is the bomb terror forgotten, which cost millions of innocent people their lives or health and all their cherished possessions? Should that not make up for what was sinned in German lands? Should the misery of the refugees which cries to Heaven not act disarmingly?"

"I came to Germany from the South Tyrol as a bride, thirty years ago. I have shared the German ordeal from the the first day to the last, taking blow after blow, making sacrifice after sacrifice, drained the bitter cup to the end— and now I feel accused, too, of things I never did."

"The misery which has now overtaken the whole nation is so gigantic, growing to such unimaginable size, that one should not rub salt into the wounds. The population, in its surely innocent parts, has already suffered more than just atonement may perhaps require."

Indeed the disaster is apocalyptical. Everyone complains, and rightly so: those who were rescued from concentration camps or persecution and still remember the frightful suffering; those who lost their dear ones in the most cruel manner; the millions of evacuees and refugees roaming the road without hope; the many hangers-on of the Party now being weeded out and suddenly in want; the Americans and other Allies who gave up years of their lives and had millions killed; the European nations tormented under the terrorist rule of the National-Socialist Germans; the German emigrants forced to live in a foreign-language environment, under the most difficult conditions. Everyone, everyone.

Everywhere the complaints turn into accusations. Against whom? In the end: all against all.

In this horrible world situation, in which at present our distress in Germany is comparatively the greatest, we must not forget the interrelation of the whole. The guilt question keeps leading back to it.

In my enumeration of complainants I put the manifold groups side by side with the intention of making the incongruity felt at once. The distress may as such, as destruction of life, be all of one kind; but it differs essentially in its general connection as well as in its particular place therein. It is unjust to call all equally innocent.

On the whole, the fact remains that we Germans—however much we may now have come into the greatest distress among the nations—also bear the greatest responsibility for the course of events until 1945.

Therefore we, as individuals, should not be so quick to feel innocent, should not pity ourselves as victims of an evil fate, should not expect to be praised for suffering. We should question ourselves, should pitilessly analyze ourselves: where did I feel wrongly, think wrongly, act wrongly—we should, as far as possible, look for guilt within ourselves, not in things, nor in the others; we should not dodge into distress. This follows from the decision to turn about, to improve daily. In doing so we face God as individuals, no longer as Germans and not collectively.

Dodging into a Generality

I feel relieved when I myself become individually unimportant because the whole is something that happens to me without my cooperation and thus without personal guilt. I live in the view of the whole, then, a mere impotent sufferer or impotent participant. I no longer live out of myself. A few examples:

(1) The moral interpretation of history as a whole lets us expect a justice on the whole—for "all guilt is on earth requited," as the poet says.

I know myself a prey to a total guilt. My own doing scarcely matters any longer. If I am on the losing side, the overall metaphysical inescapability is shattering. If I am on the winning side, my success is flavored with the good conscience of superior virtue. This tendency not to take ourselves seriously as individuals paralyzes our moral impulses. Both the pride of a self-abasing guilt confession in the one instance and the pride of moral victory in the other become evasions of the really human task which always lies in the individual.

Yet experience contradicts this total view. The course of events is not unequivocal at all. The sun shines alike upon the just and the unjust. The distribution of fortune and the morality of actions do not seem to be interconnected.

However, it would be an equally false total judgment to say, on the contrary, that there is no justice.

True, in some situations the conditions and acts of a state fill us with the ineradicable feeling that "that can't end well" and "there is bound to be a reckoning." But this feeling no sooner puts its trust in justice, beyond comprehensible human reactions to evil, than errors appear. There is no certainty. Truth and probity fail to come by themselves. In most cases amends are dispensed with. Ruin and vengeance strike the innocent along with the guilty. The purest will, complete veracity, the greatest courage may remain unsuccessful if the situation is inopportune. And many passive ones come by the favorable situation undeservedly, due to the acts of others.

In the end, such things as atonement and guilt lie only in the personality of the individuals. Despite metaphysical truth which it may contain, the idea of total guilt and being ensnared in an overall guilt-atonement relationship comes to tempt the individual to evade what is wholly and solely his business.

(2) Another total view holds that finally everything in the world comes to an end, that nothing is ever started without failing in the end, that everything contains the ruinous germ. This view puts non-success with every other non-success on the one common level of failure, and thus, in an abstraction, robs it of its weight.

(3) Interpreting our own disaster as due to the guilt of all, we give it a metaphysical weight by the construction of a new singularity. Germany is the sacrificial substitute in

the catastrophe of the age. It suffers for all. It erupts in the universal guilt, and atones for all.

There is a false pathos in this application of ideas from Isaiah and Christianity, serving in turn to divert men from the sober task of doing what is really in their power—from improvement within the sphere of the comprehensible and from the inner transformation. It is the digression into "estheticism" which by its irresponsibility diverts from realization out of the core of individual self-existence. It is a new way of acquiring a false collective feeling of our own value.

(4) We seem as though delivered from guilt if in view of the vast suffering among us Germans we cry out, "It has been atoned for."

Here we have to differentiate again. A crime is atoned for; a political liability is limited by a peace treaty and thus brought to an end. As far as these two points are concerned, the idea is correct and meaningful. But moral and metaphysical guilt, which are understood only by the individual in his community, are by their very nature not atoned for. They do not cease. Whoever bears them enters upon a process lasting all his life.

Here we Germans face an alternative. Either acceptance of the guilt not meant by the rest of the world but constantly repeated by our conscience comes to be a fundamental trait of our German self-consciousness—in which case our soul goes the way of transformation—or we subside into the average triviality of indifferent, mere living. Then no true search for God awakens any more in our amidst; then the true nature of existence is no longer revealed to us; then we no longer hear the transcendent meaning of our sublime poetry and art and music and philosophy; then all of this may, as past, perhaps become a memory of other nations— nations capable still of hearing the voice of what Germans, once upon a time, brought forth and what Germans were but are no more.

There is no other way to realize truth for the German than purification out of the depth of consciousness of guilt.

The Way of Purification

Purification in action means, first of all, making amends.

Politically this means delivery, from inner affirmation, of the legally defined reparations. It means tightening our belts, so part of their destruction can be made up to the nations attacked by Hitler Germany.

Besides the legal form assuring a just distribution of the load, such deliveries presuppose life, working ability, and working possibility. The political will to make amends must inevitably flag if political acts of the victors destroy these premises. For then we should not have a peace aimed at reparation but continued war aiming at further destruction.

There is more to reparation, however. Everyone really affected by the guilt he shares will wish to help anyone wronged by the arbitrary despotism of the lawless régime.

There are two different motivations which must not be confused. The first calls on us to help wherever there is distress, no matter what the cause—simply because it is near and calls for help. The second requires us to grant a special right to those deported, robbed, pillaged, tortured and exiled by the Hitler régime.

Both demands are fully justified, but there is a difference in motivation. Where guilt is not felt, all distress is immediately leveled on the same plane. If I want to make up for what I, too, was guilty of, I must differentiate between the victims of distress.

This way of purification by reparation is one we cannot dodge. Yet there is much more to purification. Even reparation is not earnestly willed and does not fulfill its moral purpose except as it ensues from our cleansing transmutation.

Clarification of guilt is at the same time clarification of our new life and its possibilities. From it spring seriousness and resolution.

Once that happens, life is no longer simply there to be naively, gaily enjoyed. We may seize the happiness of life if it is granted to us for intermediate moments, for breathing spells—but it does not fill our existence; it appears as amiable magic before a melancholy background. Essentially, our life remains permitted only to be consumed by a task.

The result is modest resignation. In inner action before the transcendent we become aware of being humanly finite and incapable of perfection. Humility comes to be our nature.

Then we are able, without will to power, to struggle with love in discussing truth, and in truth to join with each other.

Then we are capable of unaggressive silence—it is from the simplicity of silence that the clarity of the communicable will emerge.

Then nothing counts any longer but truth and activity. Without guile we are ready to bear what fate has in store for us. Whatever happens will, while we live, remain the human task that cannot be completed in the world.

Purification is the way of man as such. There, purification by way of unfolding the guilt idea is just one moment. Purification is not primarily achieved by outward actions— not by an outward finishing, not by magic. Rather, purification is an inner process which is never ended but in which we continually become ourselves. Purification is a matter of our freedom. Everyone comes again and again to the fork in the road, to the choice between the clean and the murky.

Purification is not the same for all. Each goes his personal way. It is not to be anticipated by anyone else, nor can it be shown. General ideas can do no more than alert, perhaps awaken.

If at this close of our discussions of guilt we ask what purification consists in, no concrete reply is possible beyond what has been said. If something cannot be realized as an end of rational will but occurs as a metamorphosis by inner action, one can only repeat the indefinite, comprehensive figures of speech: uplift by illumination and growing transparency—love of man.

As for guilt, one way is to think through the thoughts here expounded. They must not only be abstractly, mentally thought, but actually carried out; they must be recalled, appropriated or rejected with one's own being. Purification is this execution and what comes out of it. It is not something new, tacked on at the end.

Purification is the premise of our political liberty, too; for only consciousness of guilt leads to the consciousness of solidarity and co-responsibility without which there can be no liberty.

Political liberty begins with the majority of individuals in a people feeling jointly liable for the politics of their community. It begins when the individual not merely covets and chides, when he demands of himself, rather, to see reality and not to act upon the faith—misplaced in politics—in an earthly paradise failing of realization only because of the others' stupidity and ill-will. It begins when he knows, rather, that politics looks in the concrete world for the negotiable path of each day, guided by the ideal of human existence as liberty.

In short: without purification of the soul there is no political liberty.

Our progress with inner purification on the basis of guilt consciousness can be checked by our reaction to attacks.

Without guilt consciousness we keep reacting to every attack with a counterattack. Once we have been shaken by the inner tremors, however, the external attack will merely brush the surface. It may still be offensive and painful, but it does not penetrate to the interior of the soul.

Where consciousness of guilt has been appropriated, we bear false and unjust accusations with tranquillity. For pride and defiance are molten.

If we truly feel guilt, so that our consciousness of being is in transformation, reproach from others seems to us like harmless child's play, unable to hurt where the real guilt consciousness is an indelible prick and has forced a new form on self-consciousness. Reproached like this, we rather feel sorrow at the other's unconcern and unawareness. If an atmosphere of trust prevails, we may remind him of the guilt potentialities in every human being. But we can no longer get angry.

Without transillumination and transformation of our soul, sensitivity would only increase in helpless impotence. The poison of psychological transpositions would ruin us. We must be ready to put up with reproaches, must listen to and then examine them. We must seek out rather than shun attacks on us, because they enable us to check up on our own thought. Our inner attitude will stand the test.

Such purification makes us free. The course of events lies not in man's hand, though man may go incalculably far in guiding his existence. There remains uncertainty and the possibility of new and greater disasters, while no new happiness is guaranteed by the awareness of guilt and the resulting transformation of our being. These are the reasons why purification alone can free us so as to be ready for whatever comes. For only the pure soul can truthfully live in this tension: to know about the possible ruin and still remain tirelessly active for all that is possible in the world.

In regarding world events we do well to think of Jeremiah. When Jerusalem had been destroyed, state and country lost, the prophet forcibly taken along by the last few Jews who were fleeing to Egypt—when he had to see those sacrificing to Isis in the hope that she would do more for them than Jehovah, his disciple Baruch despaired. And Jeremiah answered, "The Lord saith thus: Behold; that which I have built will I break down, and that which I have planted I will pluck up, and seekest thou great things for thyself? Seek them not." What does that mean? That God is, is enough. When all things fade away, God is—that is the only fixed point.

But what is true in the face of death, in extremity, turns into a dangerous temptation if fatigue, impatience, despair drive man to plunge into it prematurely. For this stand on the verge is true only if borne by the unswerving deliberation always to seize what remains possible while life endures. Our share is humility and moderation.

At 6(6) F